LEGAL
RESEARCH
MADE EASY

LEGAL RESEARCH MADE EASY

Third Edition

Suzan Herskowitz Singer
Attorney at Law

SPHINX® PUBLISHING
AN IMPRINT OF SOURCEBOOKS, INC.®
NAPERVILLE, ILLINOIS
www.SphinxLegal.com

Third Edition, 2002
Second Printing, May 2003
Published by: **Sphinx® Publishing, An Imprint of Sourcebooks, Inc.®**

<u>Naperville Office</u>
P.O. Box 4410
Naperville, Illinois 60567-4410
630-961-3900
Fax: 630-961-2168
www.sourcebooks.com
www.SphinxLegal.com

This publication is designed to provide accurate and authoritative information in regard to the subject matter covered. It is sold with the understanding that the publisher is not engaged in rendering legal, accounting, or other professional service. If legal advice or other expert assistance is required, the services of a competent professional person should be sought.
From a Declaration of Principles Jointly Adopted by a Committee of the
American Bar Association and a Committee of Publishers and Associations

This product is not a substitute for legal advice.

Disclaimer required by Texas statutes.

Library of Congress Cataloging-in-Publication Data
Herskowitz Singer, Suzan, 1961-
     Legal research made easy / Suzan Herskowitz Singer.-- 3rd ed.
         p. cm. -- (Legal survival guides)
     Includes index.
     ISBN 1-57248-223-0 (alk. paper)
         1. Legal research--United States--Popular works. I. Title. II. Series.

     KF240 .H47 2002
     340'.07'2073--dc21
                                                                    2002021173

Printed and bound in the United States of America.
VHG Paperback — 10 9 8 7 6 5 4 3 2

CONTENTS

USING SELF HELP LAW BOOKS ix

INTRODUCTION xiii

CHAPTER 1: WHERE TO START 1
Where to Find Law Libraries
Your Legal Problem
Substantive and Procedural Law
Looking Up Procedures
Looking Up Your Rights
Legal Encyclopedias
Indices
Card Catalogs

CHAPTER 2: PRACTICE MANUALS, SPECIALTY BOOKS, AND LAW REVIEWS 13
Practice Manuals
Specialty Books
Law Reviews and Legal Periodicals

CHAPTER 3: STATUTES AND CODES. 19
The Difference Between Statutes and Codes
The Legislative Process
Sources of Statutes
How to Find a Statute
Annotations
Regulations
Attorney General Opinions

CHAPTER 4: RESEARCHING CASE LAW. 37
Case Law Defined

CHAPTER 5: SHEPARD'S CITATIONS 61
    Shepard's Citations Defined
    Which Shepard's to Use
    How to Shepardize a Case
    How to Shepardize a Statute
    Other Shepard's Applications

CHAPTER 6: AMERICAN LAW REPORTS. 75
    How to Find American Law Reports
    Updating American Law Reports

CHAPTER 7: COMPUTERIZED DATABASES 91
    CD-ROM
    Westlaw® and LexisNexis™

CHAPTER 8: LEGAL RESEARCH ON THE INTERNET 95
    Obtaining Access to the Internet
    Finding Resources on the Net Using Search Engines
    Finding Legal Resources on the Net

CHAPTER 9: PUTTING IT ALL TOGETHER 105
    Ask a Librarian
    When Enough Is Enough
    Summary of Steps for Effective Legal Research

GLOSSARY 109

APPENDIX: SAMPLE RESEARCH PROBLEM 117

INDEX 127

ACKNOWLEDGEMENTS

In this third edition, I would like to thank my former students at Keiser College in Fort Lauderdale, Florida for their comments when we used the second edition in class. They were invaluable. I would also like to thank Washington and Lee University School of Law, Wilbur C. Hall Library, in Lexington, Virginia for allowing me to use their lovely facilities for research of this edition.

My sincerest thank you to the late Iris Caldwell, my friend and reference librarian extraordinaire. Everything I learned about researching government documents, I learned from her. Thank you again to the reference staff at Nova Southeastern University, Shepard Broad Law Center Library, who assisted me with the initial research for the first and second editions.

To Joshua Gardner, Attorney at Law, who took the original first edition manuscript to a law library for a test drive while he was in college and gave me suggestions that have shaped each edition. To my friend, Harriet Gardner Eisen, who took the original manuscript on her vacation so that I could benefit from her editorial comments, suggestions and insight. Beyond the call of duty and bounds of friendship.

And to my husband, Steven B. Singer, who drove me four hours round-trip from our home to Washington and Lee, giving up his weekend so I could do research.

Suzan Herskowitz Singer
Attorney at Law

USING SELF-HELP LAW BOOKS

Before using a self-help law book, you should realize the advantages and disadvantages of doing your own legal work and understand the challenges and diligence that this requires.

THE GROWING TREND

Rest assured that you won't be the first or only person handling your own legal matter. For example, in some states, more than seventy-five percent of divorces and other cases have at least one party representing him or herself. Because of the high cost of legal services, this is a major trend and many courts are struggling to make it easier for people to represent themselves. However, some courts are not happy with people who do not use attorneys and refuse to help them in any way. For some, the attitude is, "Go to the law library and figure it out for yourself."

We at Sphinx write and publish self-help law books to give people an alternative to the often complicated and confusing legal books found in most law libraries. We have made the explanations of the law as simple and easy to understand as possible. Of course, unlike an attorney advising an individual client, we cannot cover every conceivable possibility.

COST/VALUE ANALYSIS

Whenever you shop for a product or service, you are faced with various levels of quality and price. In deciding what product or service to buy, you make a cost/value analysis on the basis of your willingness to pay and the quality you desire.

When buying a car, you decide whether you want transportation, comfort, status, or sex appeal. Accordingly, you decide among such choices as a Neon, a Lincoln, a Rolls Royce, or a Porsche. Before making a decision, you usually weigh the merits of each option against the cost.

When you get a headache, you can take a pain reliever (such as aspirin) or visit a medical specialist for a neurological examination. Given this choice, most people, of course, take a pain reliever, since it costs only pennies; whereas a medical examination costs hundreds of dollars and takes a lot of time. This is usually a logical choice because it is rare to need anything more than a pain reliever for a headache. But in some cases, a headache may indicate a brain tumor and failing to see a specialist right away can result in complications. Should everyone with a headache go to a specialist? Of course not, but people treating their own illnesses must realize that they are betting on the basis of their cost/value analysis of the situation. They are taking the most logical option.

The same cost/value analysis must be made when deciding to do one's own legal work. Many legal situations are very straight forward, requiring a simple form and no complicated analysis. Anyone with a little intelligence and a book of instructions can handle the matter without outside help.

But there is always the chance that complications are involved that only an attorney would notice. To simplify the law into a book like this, several legal cases often must be condensed into a single sentence or paragraph. Otherwise, the book would be several hundred pages long and too complicated for most people. However, this simplification necessarily leaves out many details and nuances that would apply to special or unusual situations. Also, there are many ways to interpret most legal questions. Your case may come before a judge who disagrees with the analysis of our authors.

Therefore, in deciding to use a self-help law book and to do your own legal work, you must realize that you are making a cost/value analysis. You have decided that the money you will save in doing it yourself

outweighs the chance that your case will not turn out to your satisfaction. Most people handling their own simple legal matters never have a problem, but occasionally people find that it ended up costing them more to have an attorney straighten out the situation than it would have if they had hired an attorney in the beginning. Keep this in mind if you decide to handle your own case, and be sure to consult an attorney if you feel you might need further guidance.

LOCAL RULES   The next thing to remember is that a book that covers the law for the entire nation, or even for an entire state, cannot possibly include every procedural difference of every county court. Whenever possible, we provide the exact form needed; however, in some areas, each county, or even each judge, may require unique forms and procedures. In our *state* books, our forms usually cover the majority of counties in the state, or provide examples of the type of form that will be required. In our *national* books, our forms are sometimes even more general in nature but are designed to give a good idea of the type of form that will be needed in most locations. Nonetheless, keep in mind that your *state*, county, or judge may have a requirement, or use a form, that is not included in this book.

You should not necessarily expect to be able to get all of the information and resources you need solely from within the pages of this book. This book will serve as your guide, giving you specific information whenever possible and helping you to find out what else you will need to know. This is just like if you decided to build your own backyard deck. You might purchase a book on how to build decks. However, such a book would not include the building codes and permit requirements of every city, town, county, and township in the nation; nor would it include the lumber, nails, saws, hammers, and other materials and tools you would need to actually build the deck. You would use the book as your guide, and then do some work and research involving such matters as whether you need a permit of some kind, what type and grade of wood are available in your area, whether to use hand tools or power tools, and how to use those tools.

Before using the forms in a book like this, you should check with your court clerk to see if there are any local rules of which you should be aware, or local forms you will need to use. Often, such forms will require the same information as the forms in the book but are merely laid out differently, use slightly different language, or use different color paper so the clerks can easily find them. They will sometimes require additional information.

CHANGES IN THE LAW
Besides being subject to state and local rules and practices, the law is subject to change at any time. The courts and the legislatures of all fifty states are constantly revising the laws. It is possible that while you are reading this book, some aspect of the law is being changed or a court is interpreting a law in a different way. You should always check the most recent statutes, rules and regulations to see what, if any changes have been made.

In most cases, the change will be of minimal significance. A form will be redesigned, additional information will be required, or a waiting period will be extended. As a result, you might need to revise a form, file an extra form, or wait out a longer time period; these types of changes will not usually affect the outcome of your case. On the other hand, sometimes a major part of the law is changed, the entire law in a particular area is rewritten, or a case that was the basis of a central legal point is overruled. In such instances, your entire ability to pursue your case may be impaired.

Again, you should weigh the value of your case against the cost of an attorney and make a decision as to what you believe is in your best interest.

INTRODUCTION

When most non-lawyers walk into a law library to do research, they are immediately awed by the vast array of books. The sheer number of them is intimidating, and the prospect of trying to do research in them is frightening. Digests? Case reporters? Looseleaf services? Statutes and codes? What are they? What are they for? And most importantly, how does one use them?

Most people reason that among all of those books there has to be one that will yield all the information they need. They expect that every answer to every question they have on a particular topic will be in one volume—a nice, neat little package. Unfortunately, research in a law library is not that nice or neat. It tends to take time, and only rarely will they find all the information they are seeking in one place.

Why would you do your own legal research? Perhaps your lawyer said you would save money if you helped with research. Perhaps you do not want to hire a lawyer. Perhaps you are not even sure you need a lawyer. One thing is certain, however. If you need legal information about a particular problem you must go to a law library.

Now you are standing inside that law library, looking at all of those books, and you are afraid you will never find what you are looking for.

This guide is designed to take some of that fear out of legal research. In it you will find an explanation of how to do legal research as well as descriptions of the main sources of information necessary for effective legal research. There are tables and examples of each source throughout, which will put it all in perspective. The appendix gives an example of a legal problem and how one would go about conducting research on it. This will help you "put it all together," and see how the various sources interrelate.

While this book is designed specifically for those who are not familiar with the legal system or legal research, it can be an effective tool or refresher for anyone in the profession, whether that person is a lawyer, law student, paralegal, or legal secretary.

WHERE TO START 1

A law library is a must for effective legal research. It is the only place you can go for "one stop shopping" when you have a legal problem. You may not be familiar with the "culture" of a law library. In this chapter, you will learn where to find a library and what to expect once you get there. This chapter also helps you get your feet wet by explaining how to begin the process of solving your problem.

WHERE TO FIND LAW LIBRARIES

COUNTY LAW LIBRARIES

Use your city or county public library only if a law library is unavailable in your area, or if the public library has most of the materials described in this book.

Most county governments fund a law library. Depending on the size of the county, the library collection can be small or quite extensive. It may cover a large area, or simply consist of a few shelves in an office or conference room adjacent to the judge's chambers. In almost all circumstances, the library is located within the main courthouse in the county seat. Since these libraries are publicly owned and supported by your tax dollars, they are generally open to the public during regular courthouse hours. Some may be open on selected evenings and weekends, but you cannot depend on that. They usually have a law librarian available

to offer assistance but that assistance may be limited due to staffing and time constraints. In smaller counties, the judge's secretary or law clerk may do double-duty as the "librarian."

You will usually find the phone number for the county law library in the white or blue pages of your local phone directory under the county government section. If it is not listed under a separate heading of "library" or "law library," you may find it listed as a subheading under "courthouse." If all else fails, call the main information number for the county for assistance.

LAW SCHOOL
LIBRARIES

Access to a law school library may depend on whether the law school is a public or private institution. In general, a public university law school library will have open public access. Private university law library access may be open, limited, or closed, depending upon the policy of the law library.

If you have a law school in your area, use your local white pages telephone directory to look up the university and then find the subheading for the law school. The library's main number is generally listed under "law library."

The person at the information or circulation desk of the library will be able to give you information about public access and hours. All law school libraries have restricted hours during exams and school breaks, so be sure to call if it is the end of the fall or spring semester, during the summer, or close to a holiday. Otherwise, you may get to the library and find it restricted to the public or closed. The information desk will also be able to tell you what type of librarian assistance is available. Do not be surprised if it is limited, even for public universities, since the library's main objective is to serve the students and faculty of the institution.

WHAT TO BRING
WITH YOU—
SUPPLIES AND
MONEY

There are a few items you will find necessary at the library, and you should not expect the library to supply them. One is an ample supply of paper. Scraps of paper will not suffice because you will be taking lots of notes. Also bring a supply of pens or sharpened pencils.

Legal research usually requires the use of a copy machine. When you are reading a case, you will want to make notes and highlight or under-line portions of it. You could take down the portions by hand, but after a while you will probably find it tedious and time-consuming. Most law libraries have copy machines, or at least offer library users access to one somewhere in the building. When you call the information desk for the hours of operation, make sure you inquire about the cost of making copies. Also inquire about whether the library makes change. Some do not. It is best to know in advance.

Most libraries, county and law school, have what are called "copy cards." These are plastic cards about the size of a credit card with a magnetic strip on the back. Here are some tips about copy cards and making copies:

- You pay a set price for the card, say $5.00, and you will receive a set number of copies, say sixty copies.

- When you insert the card into a reader, the card will be debited automatically each time you make a copy.

- Usually there is a discount on the price per copy if you purchase a copy card.

- If the cards are $5.00 or $10.00, or whatever price, exact change will probably be required unless the library will make change for you.

- If you must purchase the card from a machine, make sure your bills are not rumpled or the machine may reject them.

- Be aware that unless there is a problem with the copy machine, the library may not reimburse you for copies made in error.

- Always check the machine's settings before you press the copy button.

YOUR LEGAL PROBLEM

Before you pick up your first law book you must decide what your goal or goals will be. When you brainstorm about your problem, your focus—and therefore your chances of finding the right information—will improve. What follows is a guide for determining your goals.

1. Formulate a clear idea of what information you need.

Are you looking for information about your legal rights, for example at your job or in a dispute with the city? Or, do you want to perform a specific procedure such as filing a divorce or registering a trademark? If you want to perform a procedure you will need a different type of book than if you want to know your rights in a dispute.

If you want to register a trademark, for example, there will be books that explain the process in a step-by-step manner. But if you want to know if you can sue your employer for discrimination you will have to read several statutes and the decisions of many courts to see if your situation fits any of them. If you want to file for divorce you may be able to use a simple procedure book, but if there is something unusual about your case you may want to do further research into other court cases.

Also, are you looking for an answer to a specific question (such as "Can alimony be stopped if my ex-wife moves in with her boyfriend?"), or for more general information about an area of the law (such as "How do I go about getting a divorce?")

2. Think of all possible words and phrases that describe your research topic.

If you are trying to find information about child support, for example, you would think of words such as "child," "minor," "infant," "child support," "aid," "maintenance," etc. Write down all of the words you can think of and add to the list as more come to mind. A thesaurus may be helpful. Ask the librarian for a copy of *Roget's* as well as a legal thesaurus. You may also want to consult a law dictionary. Ask

for a copy of *Black's Law Dictionary* or *Ballentine's Law Dictionary*. A regular dictionary such as *Webster's* or *American Heritage* may be helpful as well.

Lastly, you may want to consult a set of books published by West Publishing Company called *Words and Phrases*. This set consists of ninety volumes of "headnote abstracts" (see Chapter 4 for discussions about headnotes and abstracts), which will furnish you with definitions of words and phrases that are legally meaningful. In brief, a *headnote* is a short summary of a legal rule of fact in a case. Using this set will not only yield synonyms, but will be helpful when you are unsure about the legal meaning of a word or phrase.

3. **Decide whether your case involves federal law or state law or both.**

Each state and the federal government have their own sets of laws. Some cases, such as divorce, are only covered by state law, and others such as copyright, are only covered by federal law. But some matters, such as discrimination, may be covered by both state and federal laws. In your preliminary research you must determine which state laws are applicable to your problem, and whether federal law applies.

How do you know what type of law you should research? Ask yourself what your problem involves. If your problem concerns the Internal Revenue Service, for example, you would be interested in federal law, but if your problem is associated with state taxation of income or obtaining a divorce, you would be interested in state law. The initial research you do will point you toward statutes or court cases. Note whether these are state or federal.

If you are researching state law, be sure you have the right state. Do not assume that the law in one state is the same as the law in another. Often the laws in the fifty states are very different from each other. Federal law, if it applies, may be very different from state law. If you think your problem may be dependent on another state's laws, or more than one state's laws, you must research each state independently.

4. Decide whether you are dealing with civil or criminal law.

Sometimes this is confusing to those people not involved daily in the legal process. How do you know if something is civil or criminal? Usually it depends upon the party entitled to bring the lawsuit.

In general, unless there is a specific statute with criminal penalties attached to it, the matter will not involve criminal law. For example, if a person owes you rent and does not pay you, or accidentally drives into the side of your house, there will probably not be a crime involved.

If there is a crime involved, and you are the victim, you will not be able to bring the criminal suit yourself. The government brings the suit, not just on your behalf, but on behalf of "the people," or all of the citizens of the state. The idea behind this is that the peace of the community was breached by the alleged acts of the defendant, so the government, as the protector of the community and its people, deals with the problem. This concept originated with English Common Law, on which the laws in the United States are based. Anyone who breached the "King's peace" was guilty of a crime, and the King, through his officials, prosecuted.

However, you may not assume that if the government is a party to a lawsuit, the action must be criminal. The government can bring a civil action also. For example, if the county wants to widen a street and needs part of your front yard, the county brings a condemnation suit using its power of eminent domain. This means the county can take your property and pay you for it. This is not a criminal action because you are not being *prosecuted* for a crime. It is a civil action only. A civil action is one not involving criminal acts and is often brought to correct what is perceived as an injury or wrong against the person bringing the lawsuit.

In many criminal cases the victim also has the right to bring a civil lawsuit for compensation, or money damages. For example, if a member of your family is murdered or injured, or if your property is criminally damaged or stolen, you can file a civil suit for damages. This suit is not part of the criminal prosecution and the state does not help you with your suit.

If you are accused of a crime you can be subject to both prosecution by the state and a civil suit by the victim. In such a situation you will need to know both the civil and criminal laws related to the matter.

Once you have completed these four steps, you can go to the books themselves and actively research your topic. If you have difficulty completing these steps, however, you will want to consult a legal encyclopedia (see page 9).

SUBSTANTIVE AND PROCEDURAL LAW

Most legal matters involve both substantive and procedural law. *Substantive* law is the law of whether or not something can be done, or what your legal "rights" are in a matter. For example, in a divorce the substantive law would tell you if you can get a divorce and what the terms of the divorce can be.

Procedural law is the law that determines which procedure you must use to obtain what you want. In a divorce it tells you which papers you must file and what they must include.

Regardless of your problem or question, the best place to start is usually with a practice manual (or self-help law book), if you can find one. If not you could start with a legal encyclopedia.

LOOKING UP PROCEDURES

If your goal is to complete a legal procedure such as filing an adoption, registering a patent or getting your security deposit back from a landlord, there may be simple explanations of these procedures available to you.

LAWBOOKS FOR CONSUMERS

In recent years there have been many books published explaining legal procedures in simple language. Many of these are available at law libraries, public libraries and bookstores. These include a simplified explanation of the law and often the forms needed to complete the procedure. These are usually thorough enough if your case is simple.

PRACTICE MANUALS FOR LAWYERS

For most states there are practice manuals explaining how to practice law to lawyers. Some of these books are published by private companies and others are published by the "continuing legal education" department of the state bar associations. Many law libraries carry these books.

They can be your most useful tool in completing a legal procedure, especially when matters are more complicated than those covered by consumer legal books. These are described in Chapter 2 of this book.

STATUTES, RULES, AND REGULATIONS

For many procedures the legal requirements are clearly spelled out in a statute, court rule or government regulation. For example, there are laws that state, "a petition for divorce must allege the following…" If you cannot find a consumer or lawyer manual on a subject, you might be able to find a statute detailing exactly what must be done. Using statutes is described in Chapter 3 of this book.

ADVANCED RESEARCH

If your legal procedure is not a simple one or if the facts of your case are unusual and do not fit the research you have done, you need to research the case law and other advanced techniques explained in Chapters 4 through 7 of this book.

LOOKING UP YOUR RIGHTS

If you are seeking to learn your legal rights in a situation or lawsuit, your research will be more detailed and you will probably need to look into case law.

SPECIALTY BOOKS

To get an overview of the subject, you should first check to see if there is a specialty book on the subject you are researching. These are described in Chapter 2.

LEGAL ENCYCLOPEDIAS

If there are no specialty books on the topic you are researching, you can start with a legal encyclopedia. Some states have their own, but other states use a national version. These are explained on the following pages.

STATUTES AND CASE LAW

After checking the specialty books and encyclopedias, you will have some statutes or cases that apply to your case. Next you will need to read these to see if they are still valid or have been amended or overruled. This is explained in Chapters 3 through 7 of this book.

LEGAL ENCYCLOPEDIAS

If you know very little about the topic you are researching and need a broader picture of the law you should check a legal encyclopedia. Perhaps you are unable to develop a clear picture of your goal or you cannot think of words and phrases to describe your topic because you are unfamiliar with the legal terminology required. You may want to use a legal encyclopedia to assist you in beginning your research.

If you live in one of the sixteen states with its own legal encyclopedia, you are in luck. These books summarize each area of law and give you the statutes and important cases that you need to start your research.

States with their own legal encyclopedias:

California	*California Jurisprudence 3d*
Florida	*Florida Jurisprudence 2d*
Georgia	*Encyclopedia of Georgia Law*
Illinois	*Illinois Law and Practice*
Indiana	*Indiana Law Encyclopedia*
Maryland	*Maryland Law Encyclopedia*
Michigan	*Michigan Law and Practice 2d*
New Jersey	*New Jersey Practice*
New York	*New York Jurisprudence 2d, Carmody Wait 2d*
Ohio	*Ohio Jurisprudence 3d*
Pennsylvania	*Pennsylvania Law Encyclopedia*
North Carolina	*North Carolina Index 4th*
Tennessee	*Tennessee Jurisprudence*
Texas	*Texas Jurisprudence 3d*
Virginia	*Jurisprudence of Virginia and West Virginia*
West Virginia	*Jurisprudence of Virginia and West Virginia*

If you do not live in one of the listed states, there are also two national legal encyclopedias, *Corpus Juris Secundum* (known as "CJS") and *American Jurisprudence 2d* (known as "Am Jur 2d"). These explain the majority rule in the United States and, on the whole, do not take individual state peculiarities into account. There are earlier versions of both of these encyclopedias (*Corpus Juris* and *American Jurisprudence*), but it would not be worthwhile to look at them since the material is outdated.

The encyclopedias geared only to a particular state, such as *Texas Jurisprudence 3rd* ("Tex Jur 3d"), outline the law in that state. In general, use only the latest edition of state encyclopedias to avoid using materials that are obsolete.

CJS, Am Jur 2d, and the state encyclopedias offer an overview of the law on a particular topic and often give references to specific court cases (this will be discussed in more detail in chapter 4), either within the text or in footnotes. These case *citations* are frequently an excellent source of materials when beginning your research.

It is important to remember, however, that encyclopedias only give the very basic, bare-bones law in a particular area. They are meant to be a starting point in legal research, not the only source of law. Legal research should never stop with a legal encyclopedia. You would miss all the fine points of the law, which are always extremely important.

Remember to write down any relevant words or phrases that you discover while reading the encyclopedia. Every new word you find could be helpful as you continue your research.

INDICES

Actual research for both cases and statutes begins in an index. Indexes (or indices) in legal materials are just like any other index you may run across in non-legal materials. They are an alphabetical listing of subject references followed by the location of that subject within the volume or volumes in which you are looking.

Look up the first word or phrase you wrote down. When you find it, make note of the location. If you cannot find the word or phrase, either go on to the next word or phrase on your list, or look up a synonym of that word. Continue in this manner until you exhaust your list.

The location may not appear familiar to you. In most non-legal materials index locations are a page, for example, "personal injury, 10." You would go to page 10 to find information on personal injury. In many legal books, however, the location is not a page number. It may be a section number, a volume number, or even a topic (such as "Personal Injury 25"). Do not let this confuse you. You proceed to the location just as if it were a page number.

Another common mistake for first-time researchers is to find a listing in an index but not realize it is a sub-entry, rather than a main entry. Legal indexes are often broken down into many minor sub-entries. For, example, under "trusts" there may be five pages of sub-entries. If you are looking for the entry for "trustee," be sure you have found the main listing for trustee, not the sub-entry of trustee under trusts or some other entry.

CARD CATALOGS

This is one source that anyone familiar with any type of library has used before. A card catalog is a system in which the materials in the library are cross-referenced by author, title, and subject.

In older libraries, the catalog will be a series of index cards (hence the term *card* catalog) in index drawers. The cards for author, title, and subject will be separated. In most libraries today, however, the card catalog has been replaced by computer, but the information is generally catalogued in the same manner. (For a detailed discussion on computerized databases, see Chapter 7.)

If you know your topic and have a list of potential words and phrases ready, you can use the subject card catalog. If you need to learn the location of a set of books, use the title catalog to obtain that location.

Be aware, however, that many law libraries do not catalog certain sets of books, such as reporters, encyclopedias and digests, which are the books you will be using the most. If you look up certain titles, such as *Corpus Juris Secundum*, and they are not in the catalog, it will be important to ask the librarian for a map of the library with the location of these materials. You may want to ask for a tour, or perhaps the library has a "self-tour" you could take to familiarize yourself with the library's layout.

PRACTICE MANUALS, SPECIALTY BOOKS, AND LAW REVIEWS 2

When an issue has been addressed before, legal authors will often make note of the facts and court decision in their books. Many times these books will offer commentary that may help you plot your course with your legal problem. Other books offer sample forms that you may find helpful to you if you must file forms with a court, as you should always file the correct forms with the correct legal language. This chapter is designed to introduce you to these materials.

PRACTICE MANUALS

If your research project involves accomplishing a particular legal procedure, the best place to find out how to do it is in a book attorneys use to learn the procedure. These books usually contain all the forms, explanations of the procedure, and even case law. They often warn you of possible problems that can come up in the procedure.

Believe it or not, law students are not taught much about how to do specific tasks. They are taught how to "think like a lawyer" and to do research. It is only after law school that lawyers learn how to prepare such things as divorce petitions and copyright applications. Many books explain how these things are done.

In some states, there are *practice manuals* published by private companies. In many states they have been published by the continuing education division of the state bar association. For subjects covered by federal law, such as copyright and bankruptcy, several books (some consisting of several volumes) are available.

SPECIALTY BOOKS

Perhaps you are lucky and know exactly what area of law you need to be researching. Most law libraries can accommodate this luck by supplying you with a specialty book, either a *monograph* or a *treatise*. Monographs and treatises are, for the most part, library terms used to describe certain types of books.

MONOGRAPHS   *Monographs* are books that only cover a very small portion of a subject. An example outside of the legal field would be a book discussing only the Civil War battle at Gettysburg, instead of covering the entire Civil War, or a book only covering Mark Twain's *Adventures of Tom Sawyer*, instead of discussing all of Mark Twain's books.

If you know the very narrow field of law you will be dealing with, you may want to consult the card catalog for a monograph.

TREATISES   *Treatises* attempt to incorporate an entire field of law within its covers. For example, a book, or set of books, regarding the Civil War from first gunshot at Ft. Sumter to surrender at Appamattox, would be a treatise, as would a book about all of Mark Twain's works.

A treatise is a very helpful tool, even if you are a novice, as long as you know with what general area of law you are dealing. If you are looking through a treatise and are having trouble locating any useful material, you may be dealing with the wrong area of law. It would be wise to begin your search in encyclopedias, cases, and statutes until you are relatively certain of what area is most important to your problem. Then, and only then, should you consult a treatise.

A few well known treatises are: *Prosser and Keeton on Torts, Calamari on Contracts, Farnsworth on Contracts, Tribe on Constitutional Law, LaFave on Criminal Law,* and *McCormick on Evidence.* Incidentally, you may hear someone refer to many of these well known treatises as *hornbooks.*

Additionally, there may be many treatises devoted strictly to your particular state's laws on a specific topic. These treatises are likely to be printed by the state bar association, are usually geared toward the legal practitioner, and often include samples of forms and pleadings necessary for practice of law in that area. It would be to your advantage to look through the library's card catalog to find these books.

While most of your research will involve only case and statute research, you will occasionally wish to get a broader view of your problem and the topic it concerns. One way is to research in law reviews and legal periodicals. (Also see Chapter 6 on using *American Law Reports.*)

LAW REVIEWS AND LEGAL PERIODICALS

If you are really lucky there will be a recent article in a law review or in a legal periodical on the subject you are researching.

Law reviews are journals published, usually quarterly, by law schools. The staff members of most law reviews are ordinarily only those law students who are in the top ten or twenty percent of their class. These students, working under the direction of a law professor, decide which articles will be published, edit the articles as necessary, and check all quotations and citations for accuracy. There is great prestige in being a member of law review, and often those students who were on law review receive the most lucrative job offers after graduation.

These reviews print articles by law professors, attorneys, members of the judiciary, and other legal scholars on subjects of current interest. Very often the viewpoints taken by the authors expand the boundaries of legal scholarship, frequently leading to new thinking on issues, and occasionally causing change in the law itself. Law reviews may be general in nature, publishing articles on a variety of topics in each issue, or they may be dedicated to specific topics only, such as women, the environment, or estate planning.

While most law review articles are written by legal professionals, law students may be contributors to reviews as well. Articles written by students are printed after the *lead* articles by the scholars and are usually titled *commentary*.

NOTE: *Any article not considered a lead article will be entitled "commentary," whether it was written by a student or a legal professional.*

Legal periodicals, on the other hand, are generally magazines and other legal-related newsletters that are not classified as law reviews. For example, the American Bar Association publishes a monthly magazine called the *ABA Journal*. This magazine is classified as a legal periodical. Periodicals may be published weekly, bi-weekly, monthly, quarterly or annually and are usually printed by state bar associations and other legal organizations. Frequent contributors to such periodicals include law professors, attorneys, and other legal scholars, just like law reviews, but most articles are much shorter and cover a topic of current interest to practitioners.

These articles usually discuss the routine side of law instead of the academic position. For example, an article in the state bar journal may be written about new changes to the code of criminal procedure and the practical influences those changes will have upon how lawyers will handle their clients' problems and lawsuits as a result. A law review article based on the same changes in the code of criminal procedure, on the other hand, would likely discuss the constitutional ramifications of the changes—a different point of view, but both may be useful to your research.

But how do you find individual articles when there are literally hundreds of law reviews and legal periodicals to choose from? In many law school libraries, the law reviews and periodicals take up an entire floor. There are three methods, all related to each other, of conducting research in law reviews and legal periodicals.

INDEX TO LEGAL PERIODICALS

The *Index to Legal Periodicals* ("ILP") is the oldest guide to law reviews and legal periodicals. The ILP, published by the H.W. Wilson Co., has been in print since before 1952, although the only volumes currently in

print are from volume 10 of 1952 on. It indexes approximately one thousand different reviews, magazines, journals, and other legal publications which are classified as reviews or periodicals.

The ILP is published in hardcover annually, from September to August, and is updated by a pamphlet each month except September. Each volume is separated into subject and author indexes, both of which are classified alphabetically. When searching in the subject index, which is where you would usually begin, you should start in the latest monthly update pamphlet and work your way backwards into the hardcover volumes. The names of each review or periodical are generally abbreviated. The front of each volume has a table explaining what each abbreviation represents. For example, "Marq.L.Rev." represents *Marquette Law Review*.

CURRENT LAW INDEX

Current Law Index ("CLI") has been published since 1980 and is currently published by Gale Group, a business unit of The Thomson Corporation. Like the *Index to Legal Periodicals* it is published annually, from January to December, and is also updated monthly. The March, June, and September issues are quarterly cumulative and the December issue is an annual supplement. It indexes over 900 law journals, legal newspapers and specialty publications from the United States, Canada, the United Kingdom, Ireland, Australia and New Zealand.

Necessarily, there is a great deal of overlap between CLI and ILP, but CLI does cover some reviews and periodicals that ILP does not. *Current Law Index* does index items a little differently than *Index to Legal Periodicals*, so if you look up a topic in one index and cannot find something helpful, you might consider looking it up in the other. What one index might list under "divorce," the other might list under "alimony." There is no way to tell unless you research in both indexes.

LEGALTRAC

Distributed by Gale Group, a business unit of the Thomson Corporation (which owns West Publishing also), *LegalTrac* is the computer database counterpart of *Current Law Index*. A disadvantage of *LegalTrac* is that it only covers articles published since 1980, so you must rely on *Index to Legal Periodicals* for articles that may be older than 1980.

The advantage of searching in this database instead of manually in the volumes of books is that you do not need to go from book to book. When you type in your subject, the CD-ROM will reference all law reviews and legal periodicals from 1980 until the last update in reverse chronological order (from the newest article to the oldest). (See Chapter 7 on computerized databases for more information on CD-ROM.)

STATUTES AND CODES 3

Often, the answer to a legal question is found in a statute. Both procedural questions and questions about your rights may be answered in detail in the statutes for many types of matters. Once you have the statute of the subject, you can check the case law for the specifics of how the statute has been interpreted.

THE DIFFERENCE BETWEEN STATUTES AND CODES

What is the difference between a statute and a code? The terms are used interchangeably by most people. Someone will say to you "there's a statute that prohibits that" and yet the book he shows you to make his point says "Code" on the cover. In practical terms, there really is no difference between a statute and a code. These are the laws passed by state legislatures. Some states call them "statutes," and other states call them "codes."

There was a distinction between the two words at one time, but today (and in this book) they are generally used interchangeably. Traditionally, *statutes* were the laws of a state in fairly random order, and a *code* was simply a set of books in which the statutes were arranged according to subject. Today, even states that call their laws "statutes" group laws of the same subject together. So, for your purposes, the difference between a statute and a code is nothing more than semantics.

What statutes represent, however, is not just semantics. Statutes are very important to your research. If your problem is governed by a particular statute or group of statutes, you will have the legal guidelines on which to base all of your research. It is important, therefore, to understand how statutes come into being.

THE LEGISLATIVE PROCESS

FEDERAL LAW

All federal laws are enacted by Congress. Congress is divided into two houses, the Senate and the House of Representatives.

At the beginning of each Congressional year, a Senator or Representative may introduce a *bill*, which is a proposal for a law. Bills are numbered sequentially (1, 2, 3, etc.) and have a prefix of "S." or "H.R.," depending on whether the bill originated in the Senate (S.) or the House of Representatives (H.R.). The bill may be subject to committee hearings, lobbying efforts, and debate on the floor. If the originating house approves the bill, it is given to the other house for consideration, where it may be subject to more hearings and debate.

If the bill passes it is sent to the President for signing. Once signed by the President, the bill becomes law. A bill also becomes law if the President neither signs nor vetoes the bill within ten days of receiving it. If the President vetoes a bill, it can only become law if the veto is overridden by a two-thirds majority of both the Senate and the House of Representatives. A bill that is not passed through the houses, signed or overridden, is not carried over to the next session of Congress. Someone must introduce the bill again and start the process all over.

STATE LAW

The process of making law in the fifty states is similar to the way laws are made in the federal government. All states have two houses in their legislatures with the exception of Nebraska, which has only one. While the names may vary, the state houses conduct business in the same manner as does the U.S. Congress.

SOURCES OF STATUTES

FEDERAL
SOURCES

Slip laws. Once a bill becomes law, it is sent to the Archivist who publishes the law through the United States Government Printing Office. As each law is passed it is printed as a *slip law*, meaning that the law is published separately and unbound. Each slip may be just a few pages or, more likely, it will be hundreds of pages long. This does not mean that the statute or statutes you need will be hundreds of pages long, however. When laws are passed, they often contain many separate statutes on the same, or similar, topics. When they are printed, they will be numbered and published as individual statutes.

Other sources for early forms of federal law include *United States Code Congressional and Administrative News* (USCANS), which is published by West Publishing, and *Advance Sheets*, published by Lawyers Co-operative Publishing (not to be confused with the advance sheets used for updating reporters as discussed in Chapter 4).

Each issue of USCANS has its own cumulative index and a Table of Laws Enacted. Initially USCANS is printed monthly in a pamphlet form. Hardbound volumes are printed at the end of the Congressional session. Lawyers Co-operative's *Advance Sheets* is substantially the same as USCANS in scope.

A looseleaf service that will include the text of certain laws passed during the prior week is *United States Law Weekly*. This service also prints selected cases of interest so you may want to consider glancing at it for case research as well. (See the section on "Looseleaf Services" in Chapter 4.)

In addition to West's *United States Code Congressional and Administrative News* and Lawyers Co-operative's *Advance Sheets*, the federal government publishes a set of books corresponding to the slip laws it publishes. United States Statutes at Large is the set of books in which slip laws are printed at the end of the congressional session. Statutes at Large has its own index.

All slip laws, whether individual or bound in books, are printed chronologically. Additionally, amendments to the original law will be in a different volume. But, unless you are looking for new federal laws, you will be using the codified versions of the statutes.

Codified versions of federal law. The laws of the federal government have been *codified*, meaning classified, making research much easier. There are three codified versions of these laws, one published by the federal government and two by private publishers.

United States Code (U.S.C.) is the official version published by the federal government. The U.S.C. is arranged into fifty *titles*. A title is the general subject matter to which the statutes are all related.

Example: Title 26 is the Internal Revenue Code and every statute contained in this title deals with taxation.

A new edition is published every six years. Cumulative supplements are printed in between. The other two versions of codified federal law are published by private publishers. Most lawyers and other legal professionals prefer to use these sets because they are generally more up to date. (The government is very slow in printing.) Also, they are indexed better and provide editorial comment.

United States Code Annotated (U.S.C.A.) is published by West Publishing Company. It is annotated (discussed in detail below) and frequently makes reference to the "topic and key number system," (see Chapter 4 for more about this system) which is helpful when trying to find court cases pertaining to a particular statute. There is a cumulative index at the end of the set, but each title has its own index as well.

Lawyers Co-operative Publishing prints the *United States Code Service* (U.S.C.S.). Like its West counterpart, U.S.C.S. makes reference to other publications Lawyers Co-operative prints and is annotated. U.S.C.S. has a cumulative index at the end of the set.

Both U.S.C.A. and U.S.C.S. are updated by monthly pamphlets, annual "pocket parts," (in the back of each volume), and total replacement of outdated volumes when necessary.

STATE SOURCES

There is little uniformity between the statutes of the various states. Most states publish slip laws, but a few do not, and the indexing of them is inconsistent.

SESSION LAWS

There is one feature that is typical for all states, however, and that is the *session law*. All states publish session laws at the end of each legislative session. Session laws are printed chronologically, usually in pamphlet form. These pamphlets may be the only avenue to find new state laws before they are formally printed in hardbound sets of statutes or codes. Indexes are usually found at the end of each pamphlet and only cover the materials in that pamphlet, although some states will publish a cumulative index as well. They may also include a table by statute number which tells you if that particular statute has been changed, and which session law contains those changes.

STATE STATUTES AND CODES

All states have statutes or codes. However, there is little uniformity between the states as to how they are set out or indexed. Research in one state will not necessarily correspond to research in another state.

Some states have unannotated official statutes, but a few annotate their own. Most states rely entirely on private publishers to print their statutes and codes. Unlike the reporter system, however, most states sanction these volumes as proper authority for state law when there is not an official set. All states have an annotated set of statutes, which are published by private companies. (Annotations are discussed later in this chapter.)

Less than half of the states use West Publishing as its publisher and roughly twenty five states employ The Michie Company. Only a handful are published by Lawyers Co-operative. Those states engaging West as their publisher have the advantage of the topic and key number system, which is an important feature for finding related case law. You will not have much choice about cross-references to other publications, however, when using state statutes. In whatever state you are researching, you generally only have one option.

HOW TO FIND A STATUTE

INDEXES

Statutes may be found directly through an index. Statutes and codes for each state have at least one index volume. Following the guidelines in Chapter 1, you should start your research by thinking of all possible words and phrases pertaining to your problem. For example, if you are looking for laws concerning alimony, you should think of—in addition to the word "alimony"—the words "support" and "divorce. " Use these words to begin your search of the index. (See Figure 1 page 29.) Notice that the index does not lead you to a page number, but to a statute number.

You may find it tempting to go directly to a code if you think you know which title or chapter applies to your problem. In fact, it will probably be in your best interest to look through the general or cumulative index first, if for no other reason than to confirm your suspicions. Sometimes you will find that the code you thought was the right one turns out not to be. An important rule of legal research is to avoid wasting time and effort. Spend the extra few minutes looking through the index. Those minutes may save you hours in the long run.

There is no comprehensive way to look up statutes in multiple jurisdictions. (However, some treatises, or even self-help law books, may have summaries of the law in various states.) If you must find out details of the law in more than one state, you will have to search each state individually. Additionally, since not all state statutes and codes are published by West Publishing, there is not the degree of uniformity that there is when researching case law. There is no guarantee that what you found in the Michigan index under "Divorce" will be under "Divorce" in the New Hampshire index.

POPULAR NAME
TABLES

Sometimes a statute will be commonly known by a name, such as "COBRA" (Consolidated Omnibus Budget Reconciliation Act) or "The Lemon Law." You may find these through a popular name table which is very often appended as a separate volume of the statute books themselves. *Shepard's Citations* (discussed in Chapter 5) also has volumes devoted to popular names. In *Shepard's*, if the name of the law is used by more than one jurisdiction, it is listed first by the federal law and then by state law.

ANNOTATIONS

It was mentioned above that both U.S.C.A. and U.S.C.S. are annotated, as are all state statutes published by private companies. *Annotations* are abstracts, or summaries, about cases construing a particular point of law. These cases interpret the statute you are researching.

You will find the abstract or abstracts directly after the text of the statute. On occasion, there may be enough abstracts concerning a particular statute to take up ten, twenty, maybe even one hundred pages. Do you read all the pages? Not necessarily. Usually, there is a small table of contents for the abstracts. In West publications they are called *Notes of Decisions*. These tables of contents will refer you to a number, and that number will refer to the place where the annotations for that very specific point begin. (See Figure 2 page 30.)

Once you look through the annotations pertaining to your statute, you can begin your case research if you have not already. If you have already done some research in the digests, the annotations in the code or statutes may lead you to cases you did not discover before.

Even if you think you have enough cases to work with, look through the annotations anyway. You may find a case that construes the statute you are using exactly. That would open up your research again, but you should not consider that a failure. Often, good legal research requires backtracking over what appears to be the same steps. Anytime you find something else that is helpful, you are ahead of the game.

REGULATIONS

Regulations are rules that are *promulgated*, or declared, by a state or federal agency. All regulations, whether state or federal, are promulgated in essentially the same manner. The method will be described in the section on federal regulations in the following section.

FEDERAL
SOURCES

Federal Register. There are many federal agencies. Some you probably have heard of include the Internal Revenue Service (I.R.S.), the Federal Aviation Administration (F.A.A.), and the Federal Communications Commission (F.C.C.). These agencies, as well as all of the others, have many rules and regulations that they use to regulate any business or organization that comes under their jurisdiction. For example, just think about all of those tax rules that you deal with each year when tax season arrives.

They get the authority to promulgate these rules from Congress, although technically all agencies fall under the Executive Branch of government, namely the President.

When Congress passes a law, it includes a short statement that says something to the effect that it authorizes "any and all other rules and regulations as may be required." This very vague and general turn of words allows the agency involved to write any rule or regulation it deems necessary to enforce the law that Congress passed. There are only two ways a regulation may be stopped. One is if Congress removes the power from the agency; for example, if the Internal Revenue Service requires that all taxpayers must file a quarterly return and Congress passes a law stating that no taxpayer must file a quarterly return, the regulation is no longer to be enforceable. The other is if a court determines that the rule is unfair or unconstitutional and commands the agency to *cease and desist* trying to enforce it.

When a regulation is first promulgated by a federal agency it is published in the *Federal Register*. (See Figure 3 on pages 31 and 32.) The *Federal Register* is published in softcover form daily, excluding Saturdays, Sundays, and federal holidays. Pages are numbered sequentially throughout the year. Each issue in a year is considered part of one volume, for example all issues for 2001 are part of Volume 66. So, how do you find new regulations in any given year when there are approximately three hundred issues, comprising of more than 50,000 pages, per year?

Each issue contains a table of contents but that would still be an unmanageable way to do research. There are two aids to help you in this process, however. One is called the *List of CFR Sections Affected ("LSA")*, which will be discussed in the next section. The other is the *CFR Parts Affected*. This is published in each issue of the *Federal Register*. You should check the last issue for each month following the last *LSA* update. For example, if the last *LSA* is June and it is now September, you need to look in the last *Federal Register* issue for July, August, and the last *Federal Register* for September that is on the library shelf. (*LSA* is discussed below.)

Code of Federal Regulations. The *Code of Federal Regulations* ("CFR") is the codified set of all regulations. It consists of softbound pamphlets covering fifty titles. (See Figure 4 on page 33.) These titles are substantially the same as those in the *United States Code*. They are updated quarterly by title. Titles 1-16 are updated January 1 of each year, titles 17-27 by April 1, titles 28-41 by July 1, and titles 42-50 by October 1.

CFR has multiple methods of aiding you in research of agency regulations. There is an index at the end of each title, as well as a cumulative index at the end of the entire set. In addition, there is the *List of CFR Sections Affected (LSA)*. This is printed monthly and lists all new regulations promulgated since the last CFR. The *LSA* will note the volume and page in the *Federal Register* of each *CFR* section changed. (See Figure 5 on page 34.)

STATE
REGULATIONS

There is no uniformity to the publication and researching of state regulations. This means that the rules and regulations of any particular state may be in pamphlet form or looseleaf form. Updating may be weekly, monthly, quarterly, or even annually. Indexing may be spotty. This is most definitely an area that you should consult with a reference librarian if you believe you require a state regulation. It should especially be noted that many law libraries only carry the regulations for the state in which they are located.

ATTORNEY GENERAL OPINIONS

This section refers specifically to those Attorney General (AG) opinions of the individual states.

The *Attorney General* is generally the highest ranking lawyer for the state government. Aside from prosecuting certain crimes and enforcing or defending the state government's rights (if you sue your state for wrongful condemnation of your property, the AG's office will handle the case on behalf of the state), the Attorney General's office will give advisory opinions.

Advisory opinions, providing interpretations of law by the Attorney General's Office, are given upon request of the state governor, state agencies, lawyers, or in some cases, private individuals, who require an interpretation of law. This is considered necessary when there are no court cases construing a particular statute, or when the cases construing a law are either contradictory or do not address the exact nature of the problem. In some states, such opinions are considered binding law in the absence of a court opinion to the contrary.

Attorney General Opinions are usually issued in slip form, although most states do eventually bind them. Indexing is commonly done either quarterly, semi-annually or annually.

MARRIAGE

MARRIAGE—Cont'd
Costs,
  Alimony and child support proceedings, 61.17
  Dissolution of marriage, post
County court judges,
  Filing and recording affidavit of marriage, 741.10
  Licenses,
    Issuance, 741.01 et seq.
    Record of license and certificate, 741.09
    Sending out licenses signed in blank, 741.03
    Signature in blank to marriage license, 741.03
    Violation of marriage license laws, 741.05
  Transmission to judge's office of certificate of person solemnizing marriage, 741.08
Crimes and offenses,
  Bigamy, 826.01
  Incest, 826.04
  Knowingly marrying husband or wife of another, 826.03
  Sentence and punishment, investigation of record for sentencing purposes, 921.231
  Violation of license laws, 741.05
Custody. Dissolution of marriage, post
Date, entry on certificate of date of marriage and return, 741.09
Debts, antenuptial debts, liability of spouse, 708.05
Deeds and conveyances,
  Equitable distribution of marital assets and liabilities, 61.075
  Separate property of wife, 708.08
Default, alimony or support payments, 61.18
Dissolution of marriage, 61.08
Discrimination economically on basis of marital status, 725.07
Dissolution of marriage, 61.001 et seq.
  A vinculo matrimonii, 61.031
  Abolition, certain defenses, 61.044
  Abuse of spouses, custody of minor children, evidence, 61.13
  Accident and health insurance, children and minors, 61.13
  Age, alimony determination, 61.08
  Agreements,
    Antenuptial agreements, 61.052
    Support or alimony agreements, modification, 61.14
  Alimony, 61.052, 61.08
    Attachment, amounts due, 61.12
    Attorney fees, 61.16, 61.17

MARRIAGE—Cont'd
Dissolution of marriage—Cont'd
  Alimony—Cont'd
    Bankruptcy exemption, 222.201
    Bond for payment, 61.18
    Central depository, payments, 61.181
    Chancery jurisdiction, 61.011
    Checks, insufficient funds, 61.181
    Contempt, 61.18
    Costs, 61.16, 61.17
    Default in payment, 61.18
    Definitions, 61.046
    Delinquency, income deduction orders, 61.1301
    Delinquent payments, enforcement, 61.181
    Depositories, 61.181
      Defined, 61.046
    Deposits in court, 61.18
    Enforcement, 61.17
      Income deduction orders, 61.1301
      Reciprocity, 88.011 et seq.
    Execution for nonpayment, 61.18
    Expenses, 61.17
    Fees, collection, central depository, 61.181
    Garnishment, amount due, 61.12
    Income, defined, 61.046
    Income deduction orders, 61.1301
    Injunction to secure payment, 61.11
    Judgments and orders, enforcement, 61.17
    Jurisdiction, 48.193, 61.011
    Modification of judgment or agreement, 61.14
    Ne exeat to secure payment, 61.11
    Nonpayment, contempt, 61.18
    Payments, central depository, 61.181
    Pendente lite, 61.071
    Permanent alimony, 61.08
    Reciprocity, enforcement, 88.011 et seq.
    Rehabilitative alimony, 61.08
    Security, 61.08
    Service of process, 48.193
    Suit money, 61.16
    Temporary alimony, 61.071
    Withholding, income deduction orders, 61.1301
  Annuities, 61.076
  Antenuptial agreements, 61.052
  Appeal, application of law, 61.191
  Application of law, 61.191
  Arbitration and award, 61.183
  Arrearages,
    Alimony, 61.08
    Support, 61.13

§ 61.076

Note 6

tal asset contingent upon husband's survival. Rogers v. Rogers, App. 2 Dist., 622 So.2d 96 (1993).

In dividing marital asset pension upon dissolution of marriage, court should either reduce pension benefit to present value and award lump-sum or direct that part of each pension payment be paid to recipient spouse at time of payment. Rogers v. Rogers, App. 2 Dist., 622 So.2d 96 (1993).

7. Military retirement benefits

That portion of husband's future military pension which accrued during marriage was marital asset, subject to equitable distribution. Cunning-So.2d 632 (1993).

CIVIL PRACTICE AND PROCEDURE

ham v. Cunningham, App. 1 Dist., 623 So.2d 124 (1993).

Trial court abused its discretion in awarding wife percentage of husband's military retirement payments to begin when husband was eligible to retire, even if he continued on active military duty beyond that date, where parties' stipulation provided that she would receive share of retirement after such time as husband retired, stipulation was clear, there was no finding that it needed to be clarified or modified. Bissell v. Bissell, App. 1 Dist., 622 So.2d 632 (1993).

61.08. Alimony

(1) In a proceeding for dissolution of marriage, the court may grant alimony to either party, which alimony may be rehabilitative or permanent in nature. In any award of alimony, the court may order periodic payments or payments in lump sum or both. The court may consider the adultery of either spouse and the circumstances thereof in determining the amount of alimony, if any, to be awarded. In all dissolution actions, the court shall include findings of fact relative to the factors enumerated in subsection (2) supporting an award or denial of alimony.

(2) In determining a proper award of alimony or maintenance, the court shall consider all relevant economic factors, including but not limited to:

(a) The standard of living established during the marriage.

(b) The duration of the marriage.

(c) The age and the physical and emotional condition of each party.

(d) The financial resources of each party, the nonmarital and the marital assets and liabilities distributed to each.

(e) When applicable, the time necessary for either party to acquire sufficient education or training to enable such party to find appropriate employment.

(f) The contribution of each party to the marriage, including, but not limited to, services rendered in homemaking, child care, education, and career building of the other party.

(g) All sources of income available to either party.

The court may consider any other factor necessary to do equity and justice between the parties.

(3) To the extent necessary to protect an award of alimony, the court may order any party who is ordered to pay alimony to purchase or maintain a life insurance policy or a bond, or to otherwise secure such alimony award with any other assets which may be suitable for that purpose.

(4)(a) With respect to any order requiring the payment of alimony entered on or after January 1, 1985, unless the provisions of paragraph (c) or paragraph (d) apply, the court shall direct in the order that the payments of alimony be made through the appropriate depository as provided in s. 61.181.

(b) With respect to any order requiring the payment of alimony entered before January 1, 1985, upon the subsequent appearance, on or after that date, of one or both parties before the court having jurisdiction for the purpose of modifying or enforcing the order or in any other proceeding related to the order, or upon the application of either party, unless the provisions of paragraph (c) or paragraph (d) apply, the court shall modify the terms of the order as necessary to direct that payments of alimony be made through the appropriate depository as provided in s. 61.181.

(c) If there is no minor child, alimony payments need not be directed through the depository.

(d)1. If there is a minor child of the parties and both parties so request, the court may order that alimony payments need not be directed through the depository. In this case, the order of support shall provide, or be deemed to provide, that either party may subsequently

§ 61.08

apply to the depository to require that payments be made through the depository. The court shall provide a copy of the order to the depository.

2. If the provisions of subparagraph 1. apply, either party may subsequently file with the depository an affidavit alleging default or arrearages in payment and stating that the party wishes to initiate participation in the depository program. The party shall provide copies of the affidavit to the court and the other party or parties. Fifteen days after receipt of the affidavit, the depository shall notify all parties that future payments shall be directed to the depository.

3. In IV-D cases, the IV-D agency shall have the same rights as the obligee in requesting that payments be made through the depository.

Amended by Laws 1986, c. 86-220, § 115, eff. Oct. 1, 1986; Laws 1988, c. 88-98, § 2, eff. Oct. 1, 1988; Laws 1991, c. 91-246, § 3, eff. July 1, 1991.

Historical and Statutory Notes

Laws 1986, c. 86-220, § 115, eff. Oct. 1, 1986, rewrote subsec. (4).

Laws 1988, c. 88-98, § 2, eff. Oct. 1, 1988, substituted in the third sentence of subsec. (1) "either spouse and the circumstances thereof in determining" for "a spouse and the circumstances thereof in determining whether alimony will be awarded to each spouse and", and inserted at the end of subsec. (2)(d) "and the marital assets and liabilities distributed to each".

Laws 1988, c. 88-98, § 4, provides that the act "applies to all proceedings commenced after the effective date of this act."

Laws 1991, c. 91-246, § 3, eff. July 1, 1991, added the fourth sentence to subsec. (1); inserted "the nonmarital" in par. (d) and added par. (g) to subsec. (2).

Forms

See West's Florida Legal Forms, Domestic Relations.

Law Review Commentaries

All quiet on the domestic front. Gavin K. Letts, 59 Fla.Bar J. 17 (1985).

Beyond individual privacy: A new theory of family rights. Lane Rutherford, 39 U.Fla.L.Rev. 627 (1987).

Doctrine of necessaries: Contemporary application as a support remedy. 19 Stetson L.Rev. (Fla.) 661 (1990).

Gender bias in Florida's justice system. Robert Craig Waters, Ricki Lewis Tunnen and Gail Freeman, 64 Fla.BJ. 10 (May 1990).

Potential impact of AIDS. Shelly M. Mitchell, 61 Fla.B.J. 57 (Oct. 1987).

Towards the elimination of gender bias in the Florida courts. Sandy Karlan, 11 Nova L.Rev. 1669 (1987).

WESTLAW Electronic Research

See WESTLAW Electronic Research Guide following the Preface.

Notes of Decisions

Adultery, need and ability to pay 10.6
Age of spouse, lump sum alimony 134.5
Amount, rehabilitative alimony 74.5
Arrearages, jurisdiction 215.5
Automatic reduction 255
Bank accounts, lump sum alimony 118.5
Coercion, antenuptial agreements 52.5
Credits, lump sum alimony 113.5
Deferred compensation savings plan, lump sum alimony 1275
Distribution of marital assets, permanent alimony 95.4
Earning capacity, need and ability to pay 11.5
Education expenses, rehabilitative alimony 78.5
Evidence, need and ability to pay 10.5

Expenses, need and ability to pay 12.5
Future occurrences, need and ability to pay 21.5
Herpes, health care, permanent alimony 104
Income of successor spouse, need and ability to pay 14.5
Increase in alimony, adultery 34.5
Judgments and orders, temporary alimony 164.5
Loss of alimony from previous divorce 9?
Lump sum payments, rehabilitative alimony 88.6
Medical expenses 144.5
Modification, permanent alimony 97.5
Nonmarital assets, lump sum alimony 116.7
Permanent periodic alimony, insurance 20?

Presidential

Government agencies and employees:
  Government reform (Memorandum of July 11, 2001), 37105
Groom Lake, NV, Air Force's operating location near; classified information (Presidential Determination No. 2001-27), 50807
Immigration; migration and refugee assistance (Presidential Determination No. 2001-22 of July 26, 2001), 40107
India; authorization of transfer of certain U.S.-origin helicopter parts from the United Kingdom (Presidential Determination No. 2001-11), 8503
International financial institutions; withholding of funds (Presidential Determination No. 2001-08), 1561
Iran—
  Continuation of national emergency (Notice of March 13, 2001), 15013
  State of emergency (Notice of November 9, 2001), 56966
Iraq; continuation of emergency (Notice of July 31, 2001), 40105
Ireland, International Fund for; U.S. contributions (Presidential Determination No. 2001-14), 27825
Jerusalem Embassy Act; suspension of limitations (Presidential Determination No. 2001-19), 225, 34355
Korean Peninsula Energy Development Organization; U.S. contribution (Presidential Determination No. 2001-21 of July 4, 2001), 2193, 37111
Latin American Development Act of 1960; delegation of responsibility (Memorandum of May 30, 2001), 30629
Libya; continuation of emergency (Notice of January 4, 2001), 1250
Mexico City Policy, restoration (Memorandum of March 28, 2001), 17303
Middle East peace process; state of emergency (Notice of January 19, 2001), 7373
Migration and Refugee Assistance Act of 1962; availability of funds (Presidential Determination No. 2001-05 of December 15, 2000), 223
Military tribunals for non-citizens involved in terrorism activities; authorization (Military Order of November 13, 2001), 57833
Morocco-U.S. atomic energy agreement; amendment (Pres. Determination No. 01-25), 46695
Narcotics and drugs:
  Certification for major illicit drug producing and drug transit countries (Presidential Determination No. 2001-12), 14454
Nuclear-related sanctions; waiver for India and Pakistan (Presidential Determination No. 2001-28), 50095
Pakistan—
  Financial assistance (Presidential Determination No. 2002-02 of October 16, 2001), 51293, 53503
  Waiver of sanctions on export of select U.S. Munitions List U.S.-origin parts and ammunition (Presidential Determination No. 2001-23), 44521
Palestine Liberation Organization—
  Waiver and certification of statutory provisions (Presidential Determination No. 2001-13), 20585
  Waiver of statutory provisions (Presidential Determination No. 2002-03 of October 16, 2001), 53505
Refugee and migration assistance funding (Presidential Determination No. 2001-10), 8501

Russia, cooperative projects with; delegation of authority to transmit reports (Memorandum of March 3, 2000), 3851
Russian Federation; blocking Government property relating to disposition of highly enriched uranium from nuclear weapons (Notice of June 11, 2001), 32207
Security Assistance Act of 2000; delegation of reporting authority (Memorandum of May 31, 2001), 31833
Serbia and Montenegro; certification to waive application of restrictions on assistance (Presidential Determination No. 2001-07 of December 19, 2000), 1013
Sudan; state of emergency (Notice of October 31, 2001), 55869
Taiwan; trade relations (Memorandum of November 9, 2001), 57359
Transportation; modification of moratorium on certificates or permits for motor carriers of foreign contiguous countries (Memorandum of June 5, 2001), 30799
Tunisia; military drawdown (Pres. Determination No. 01-24), 46693
Vietnam—
  Continuation of waiver authority under the Trade Act of 1974 (Presidential Determination No. 2001-17), 30633
  Cooperation in accounting for U.S. prisoners of war and missing in action (Presidential Determination No. 2001-15), 27827
  Normal Trade Relations (Presidential Determination No. 2001-18), 34353
Weapons of mass destruction; continuation of emergency (Notice of November 9, 2001), 56965
Yugoslavia, Federal Republic of, Bosnian Serbs, and Kosovo; continuation of emergency (Notice of May 24, 2001), 29007

Presidio Trust

PROPOSED RULES
Semi-annual agenda, 26384
NOTICES
Environmental statements; availability, etc.:
  Presidio Trust Implementation Plan—
    Comment request, 46296
    Hearings, 39058, 48299
Meetings, 22622, 43921, 45344
  Board of Directors, 9112
Wireless telecommunications facilities sites; applications:
  Verizon Wireless, 44182

Prisons Bureau

RULES
Inmate control, custody, care, etc.:
  National security; prevention of acts of violence and terrorism, 55062

Program Support Center

NOTICES
Agency information collection activities:
  Proposed collection; comment request, 7764
  Submission for OMB review; comment request, 23946
Organization, functions, and authority delegations:
  Customer Relations Office; name change from Marketing Office, 48684
  Information Resources Management Service, 31240

Public Debt Bureau

See Fiscal Service

NOTICES
Agency information collection activities:
  Proposed collection; comment request, 9631, 9632, 9633, 9634, 19833, 23319, 23320, 23321, 23322, 55039, 55729
Privacy Act:
  Systems of records. 28222

Public Health Service

See Agency for Healthcare Research and Quality
See Agency for Toxic Substances and Disease Registry
See Centers for Disease Control and Prevention
See Food and Drug Administration
See Health Resources and Services Administration
See Indian Health Service
See National Institutes of Health
See Substance Abuse and Mental Health Services Administration

RULES
Medicaid:
  Health Care Financing Administration; agency name change to Centers for Medicare & Medicaid Services; technical amendments, 39450
Medicare:
  Health Care Financing Administration; agency name change to Centers for Medicare & Medicaid Services; technical amendments, 39450

NOTICES
Meetings:
  National Toxicology Program—
    Alternative Toxicological Methods Advisory Committee, 46020, 49196
    Genetically modified foods; allergenic potential assessment; workshop, 43021, 56839
    Scientific Counselors Board, 17724, 23037, 47237
    Up-and-Down Procedure Peer Review Panel, 36294
  National Toxicology Program:
    Carcinogens Report, Ninth Edition—
      Agents, substances, or mixtures newly listed, upgraded, or delisted, 29340
    Carcinogens Report, Tenth Edition—
      Agents, substances, mixtures, and exposure circumstances for listing or delisting, 13334
    Carcinogens Report, Eleventh Edition—
      Agents, substances, mixtures, and exposure circumstances; listing; comment request, 38430
    Center for Evaluation of Risks to Human Reproduction—
      Methanol Expert Panel report; comment request; and meeting, 37047
    Chemicals nominated for toxicological studies; testing recommendations; comment request, 38717
    In vitro estrogen and androgen receptor binding and transcriptional activation assays for endocrine disruptor screening; independent peer review evaluation, 16278

57833

Federal Register

Vol. 66, No. 222

Friday, November 16, 2001

Presidential Documents

Title 3—

The President

Military Order of November 13, 2001

Detention, Treatment, and Trial of Certain Non-Citizens in the War Against Terrorism

By the authority vested in me as President and as Commander in Chief of the Armed Forces of the United States by the Constitution and the laws of the United States of America, including the Authorization for Use of Military Force Joint Resolution (Public Law 107–40, 115 Stat. 224) and sections 821 and 836 of title 10, United States Code, it is hereby ordered as follows:

Section 1. *Findings.*

(a) International terrorists, including members of al Qaida, have carried out attacks on United States diplomatic and military personnel and facilities abroad and on citizens and property within the United States on a scale that has created a state of armed conflict that requires the use of the United States Armed Forces.

(b) In light of grave acts of terrorism and threats of terrorism, including the terrorist attacks on September 11, 2001, on the headquarters of the United States Department of Defense in the national capital region, on the World Trade Center in New York, and on civilian aircraft such as in Pennsylvania, I proclaimed a national emergency on September 14, 2001 (Proc. 7463, Declaration of National Emergency by Reason of Certain Terrorist Attacks).

(c) Individuals acting alone and in concert involved in international terrorism possess both the capability and the intention to undertake further terrorist attacks against the United States that, if not detected and prevented, will cause mass deaths, mass injuries, and massive destruction of property, and may place at risk the continuity of the operations of the United States Government.

(d) The ability of the United States to protect the United States and its citizens, and to help its allies and other cooperating nations protect their nations and their citizens, from such further terrorist attacks depends in significant part upon using the United States Armed Forces to identify terrorists and those who support them, to disrupt their activities, and to eliminate their ability to conduct or support such attacks.

(e) To protect the United States and its citizens, and for the effective conduct of military operations and prevention of terrorist attacks, it is necessary for individuals subject to this order pursuant to section 2 hereof to be detained, and, when tried, to be tried for violations of the laws of war and other applicable laws by military tribunals.

(f) Given the danger to the safety of the United States and the nature of international terrorism, and to the extent provided by and under this order, I find consistent with section 836 of title 10, United States Code, that it is not practicable to apply in military commissions under this order the principles of law and the rules of evidence generally recognized in the trial of criminal cases in the United States district courts.

(g) Having fully considered the magnitude of the potential deaths, injuries, and property destruction that would result from potential acts of terrorism against the United States, and the probability that such acts will occur, I have determined that an extraordinary emergency exists for national defense

during implementation of SCATANA. The appropriate military authority will, except under actual emergency air defense situations, ensure that such air NAVAIDS within their area of responsibility remain in operation. Control of LORAN C will be in accordance with the JCS Master Navigation Plan (SM 525-XX). If actual emergency air defense situations require shutdown of these air NAVAIDS, the appropriate military authority will immediately notify the respective commander of the affected major command of the shutdown.

§ 245.4 Application of Emergency Security Control of Air Traffic (ESCAT).

(a) *Situation.* Emergency conditions exist which threaten national security but do not warrant the declaration of Defense Emergency, Air Defense Emergency or the control of air NAVAIDS.

(b) *Intention.* To provide for the most effective use of airspace in the affected area by:

(1) Ensuring that the position of all friendly air traffic is known and can be contacted by radio, if necessary.

(2) Controlling the density of air traffic operating in airspace critical to the conduct of air defense operations.

(c) *Application.* (1) The appropriate military authority will take the following actions:

(i) Direct the affected ARTCCs to apply ESCAT.

(ii) Specifically define the affected area.

(iii) Define the types of restrictions to be placed in effect. These may require the diverting and rerouting of traffic, the restricting of traffic to certain areas or corridors, and the initiating of a requirement to obtain a Security Control Authorization prior to take-off.

(iv) Within NORAD, the region commander will advise CINCNORAD who will then advise the Administrator, FAA and the Defense Commissioner, FCC, that ESCAT has been applied. Outside NORAD the appropriate military authority will advise the Administrator, FAA and the Defense Commissioner, FCC directly. When time is vital notification may occur after ESCAT has been implemented.

(v) Direct the appropriate ARTCCs to relax or terminate restrictions as the tactical situation allows.

(2) ARTCCs will take the following actions when directed to apply ESCAT:

(i) Disseminate ESCAT instructions and restrictions received to air traffic, civil and military air traffic control facilities, flight service stations and other appropriate aeronautical facilities.

(ii) Impose the restrictions on air traffic as directed by the appropriate military authority. The restrictions will automatically include instructions for all VFR traffic to land at the nearest suitable airport and file an IFR/DVFR flight plan.

(iii) Civil and military air traffic control facilities, and other aeronautical facilities will disseminate to air traffic and aircraft operators, and will implement, those instructions and restrictions received from the ARTCCs. When an IFR or DVFR flight plan has been filed, it will be examined by the appropriate aeronautical facility to ensure that it conforms with the ESCAT restrictions placed in effect by the appropriate military authority. When a flight plan does conform with the ESCAT restrictions, the appropriate aeronautical facility will grant a Security Control Authorization and the flight can then be given take-off clearance. When a flight plan does not conform with the ESCAT restrictions, a Security Control Authorization will not be given and take-off clearance will be denied.

(iv) The pilot in command will take the following actions when ESCAT is applied:

(a) If airborne, comply with the instructions issued by the appropriate aeronautical facility.

(b) If not airborne, file an IFR or DVFR flight plan prior to take-off and comply with the instructions issued by the appropriate aeronautical facility.

(c) Aircraft which are not radio equipped may not file an IFR or DVFR flight plan and will not be permitted to operate in areas affected by ESCAT.

Figure 5: List of CFR Sections Affected (LSA)

CHANGES JULY 2, 2001 THROUGH DECEMBER 31, 2001

TITLE 31 Chapter V—Con.

515.560 Revised; interim.................36688
535.215 (a) revised; interim 38554
535.333 Revised; interim.................38554
538 Authority citation revised........36688
538.205 Revised; interim................36688
538.211 (b) through (e) redesig-
    nated as (c) through (f); new
    (b) added; interim...................36688
538.405 (b) revised; interim...........36688
538.523 Revised; interim.................36688
538.524 Removed; interim...............36689
538.525 Heading and (d) revised;
    (e) added; interim...................36689
538.526 Heading, (a), (b) introduc-
    tory text, (1) and (2) revised;
    interim 36689
539 Authority citation amended
   57381
    Appendix I amended 57381
540 Revised 38555
550 Authority citation revised........36690
550.306 Revised; interim................36690
550.308 Revised, interim.................36690
550.318 Revised; interim................36690
550.405 (b) revised; interim............36690
550.569 Revised; interim................36690
550.571 Removed; interim...............36691
    Heading and (d) revised; new
    (e) added; interim...................36691
550.572 Heading, (a), (b) introduc-
    tory text, (1) and (2) revised;
    interim 36691
550.573 Revised; interim................36692
560 Authority citation revised........36692
560.405 (b) revised; interim............36692
560.520 Heading revised; interim
   36692
560.530 Revised; interim................36692
560.531 Removed; interim..............36693
560.532 Heading and (d) revised;
    (e) added; interim...................36693
560.533 Heading, (a), (b) introduc-
    tory text, (1) and (2) revised;
    interim 36693
586 Authority citation revised.......50508
586.201 (a) note, (b) note and (d)
    note added; (c) and endnote
    revised; interim.......................50509
586.204 Note added; interim 50509
586.302 Revised; interim................50509
586.319 Revised; interim................50509
586.405 Revised; interim................50509
586.406 (a) amended; interim..........50509
586.501 Amended; interim 50509
586.517 Added; interim 50509
586.518 Added; interim 50509

586.519 Added; interim 50510
586.701 Revised; interim................50510
586.702 Revised; interim.................50510
586.703 Revised; interim................50510
586.704 Revised; interim................50511
586.705 Revised; interim................50511
587 Added; interim.........................50511
Chapter V Appendix A amended
    ....54404, 57373, 57379—57381
    Appendix B amended 57373

Proposed Rules:

1.................................54175, 59754
103...............................67670, 67685
104...............................67460
356...............................38600

TITLE 32—NATIONAL DEFENSE
Chapter I—Office of the Secretary of Defense (Parts 1—399)

3 Revised 57383
40 Removed..................................53958
42 Removed..................................53958
46 Removed..................................53958
51 Removed..................................53958
55 Removed..................................53958
62 Removed..................................53958
63 Removed..................................53958
65 Removed..................................53958
72 Removed..................................53958
76 Removed..................................53958
79 Removed..................................53958
89 Removed..................................53958
98 Removed..................................53958
102 Removed 53958
103 Removed 53958
111 Removed 53958
114 Removed 53958
115 Removed 53958
132 Removed 53958
153 Added....................................45169
157 Removed 53958
159 Removed 53958
159a Removed 53958
171 Removed 53958
186 Removed 53958
188 Removed 53958
194 Removed 53958
199.2 Amended; interim........40606, 45172
199.3 (b)(2)(i)(D), (f)(3)(vi), (3)(vii)
    and note revised; interim........40606
199.8 (c)(4) added; (d)(1) revised;
    interim 40607
199.10 (a)(1)(ii) revised; interim
   40607

DECEMBER 2001   **87**

CHANGES JULY 2, 2001 THROUGH DECEMBER 31, 2001

199.14 (h)(1)(iv)(D) and (E) added
.... 45172
199.15 (a)(6) revised; interim 40608
199.17 (a) introductory text,
    (6)(i), (ii), (b) introductory
    text, (1), (c) introductory
    text, (3), (4), and (v) revised;
    (m)(2)(iii) and (4)(iii) re-
    moved; interim.......................40608
230 Revised 46373
231 Revised 46708
231.5 (g)(5)(i) through (ix) cor-
    rected....................................54136
231.8 Heading correctly revised
.... 54136
231.9 Heading, (a) through (p)(1),
    (2) and (q) through (cc) cor-
    rectly designated...................54136
231a Removed 46374
311.5 (a)(7)(ii) revised 41780
311.8 (c)(7) added 41780
320 Revised 52681
323 Footnotes 1 through 8 revised
.... 41781
323.2 (e) revised...........................41781
323.4 (a)(1) introductory text, (2)
    introductory text, (3) and
    (b)(4) revised; (a)(1)(v) added
.... 41781
323.5 (b)(3)(iv), (4), (5), (c)(5)(ii),
    (6) introductory text, (i),
    (f)(3), (h)(6), (i)(5)(ii), (j)(5),
    (k), (1)(1), (2) and (3) revised;
    (b)(3)(v) removed 41781
323.6 Revised...............................41782
323 Appendices A and B amended
.... 41782
326.5 (j)(11) added 41783
326.17 (e) added 41783
    (f) and (g) added....................54926

Chapter V—Department of the Army (Parts 400—699)

505.5 (e)(1), (5), (6), (12), (19), (29)
    introductory text, (i), (ii),
    (31) introductory text, (i),
    (ii) and (32) revised..................55876
619 Removed 65652
668 Removed 36711

Chapter VI—Department of the Navy (Parts 700—799)

701.118 (v) and (w) added 54928
706.2 Table Three amended.............53523
    Table Four amended 53524

Table Five amended 53533
Tables Four and Five amended
.... 53525, 53526, 53527, 53530, 53531,
                                    53532
Tables Two and Five amended
.... 53528
Table Two amended...................53529
Regulation at 66 FR 53528 eff.
    date corrected 56383

Chapter VII—Department of the Air Force (Parts 800—1099)

806b Appendix C amended...............54930

Proposed Rules:

3..58422
199..39699
320..41811
326..43138
505..............................41814, 43818
701..43141
806b..43820
808..36523

TITLE 33—NAVIGATION AND NAVIGABLE WATERS

Chapter I—Coast Guard, Department of Transportation (Parts 1—199)

84.25 Added 55091
100 Temporary regulations list
.... 56035
100.35–T05–029 Added (temporary)
.... 34828
100.35–T05–030 Added (temporary)
.... 34824
100.35–T05–031 Added (temporary)
.... 34820
100.35–T05–032 Added (temporary)
.... 34826
100.35T–05–038 Added (temporary)
.... 41144
100.35T–05–040 Added (temporary)
.... 41142
100.35T–05–041 Added (temporary)
.... 41140
100.35–T05–047 Added (temporary)
.... 44052
100.35–T05–053 Added (temporary)
.... 46378
100.35–T05–055 Added (temporary)
.... 46376
100.35–T05–057 Added (temporary)
.... 47385

RESEARCHING CASE LAW 4

If your question has not been answered, or your problem has not been solved, at this juncture you will need to research actual case law.

CASE LAW DEFINED

Case law refers to the written opinions of judges in specific lawsuits. These opinions, or court decisions, are published in books called *reporters*. Generally the only opinions that are published in reporters are appellate court decisions. This means that a case will not have an opinion printed in a reporter if the case only went as far as the trial court. Very often the trial court decision will not even be written.

All cases, both civil and criminal, begin in a *trial court*, or the court where the facts and legal issues are first determined during a lawsuit. In the trial court, the case may end in a *plea bargain* or negotiation between a prosecutor and a defendant allowing a defendant to plead guilty and receive a lesser punishment (in a criminal case). It could end in *settlement* as when parties to a lawsuit come to an agreement. Or, it could end in *dismissal* without trial, meaning that the judge discharges the lawsuit. Or, a trial may be held with or without a jury. The trial court is known by many names, depending on the state or jurisdiction, what area of law is involved, and how much money is involved.

See Figure 6 on page 53 for a diagram of the state and federal court systems. The federal system is fairly simple, but the state systems can become a bit more complicated. As you can see from Figure 6, names for state courts (especially state trial courts) can vary greatly. Examples are given for some of the states that use each of the various titles. This is not a complete listing, and some states use more than one title depending upon the type of case involved or even the county in which the court is located. For example, in Virginia, depending upon the location of the court, divorce cases may be heard in either Circuit Court, Domestic Relations Court, or Experimental Family Court. Other states may have subdivisions, such as "Circuit Court, Probate Division."

In many states there are actually two levels of trial court, depending upon the amount of money in dispute, or the type of case. For example, Michigan has District Courts, which primarily handle civil cases involving less than $25,000, and criminal misdemeanor cases. Civil cases involving more than $25,000 or criminal felonies are handled in the Circuit Courts. Furthermore, some cases in the District Courts may be appealed to the Circuit Court. Therefore, the Circuit Court acts mostly as a trial court, but occasionally as an appellate court. To further complicate matters, some state court cases may also be appealed to the federal court.

If one party does not agree with the trial court's decision (or even a settlement reached without a trial), he or she may appeal it to a higher court, called an *appellate court*. These decisions are usually written and are published. You should know that most cases are not appealed. Many people do not want to spend the money on an appeal, which can be quite costly as well as time-consuming, or they may feel that they do not have a clearly appealable issue. So, many cases are not printed.

Only those cases that are printed in a reporter are considered important for legal research. Unless a case decision is printed it does not have much weight in the legal system.

PRECEDENT   Only printed cases have weight in the legal system because case law sets precedent. *Precedent* means that the court's opinion furnishes an example, or authority, for an identical or similar case based on a similar question of law. Precedent can help you select a course of action for your situation. If there is precedent for your circumstances, your position will be strengthened.

You will want to find the most recent case displaying the precedent for your particular problem. For example, if you find a case from 1958 supporting your position but a 1989 case contradicts your position, you have an obstacle you must overcome. Conversely, if the 1989 opinion supports your position, you will be in a strong position.

If you find a case that is identical to yours in every way, the case is said to be *on all fours* or *on point*. This is the best kind of case you could find in your research, but unfortunately, cases that mirror yours are hard to find. You will likely find more cases that are only marginally on point. They may have some elements that are the same as your problem and a few that are similar, while the rest of the case is not related. These cases may still be useful, especially if you can show that the situations are similar and draw analogies.

You will find many more cases that, while the area of law is identical, the situations are totally different. Do not try to compare apples and oranges if you find cases like that. Remember them if they describe the area of law well, but otherwise, you will be better off looking for cases with more similarities.

One other consideration must be given to the cases you find in your research. This is whether the case is *binding precedent* or *persuasive precedent*. Binding precedent means that the court *must* follow it. Usually each trial court is "under" a certain appellate court. The decisions of that appellate court must be followed by the trial court.

Example: Suppose your case is in a federal district court in Florida. The federal district courts in Florida are under the U.S. Court of Appeals for the Eleventh Circuit, which also covers Alabama

and Georgia. If the case you found is from the Eleventh Circuit, it is binding precedent which must be followed by the federal district court in Florida. On the other hand, if the case you found is from the U.S. Court of Appeals for the Second Circuit (which covers Connecticut, New York and Vermont), it is not binding on the Florida federal district court.

In this last instance, it is only *persuasive precedent*. That is, you can use it to argue that it is a good way to view the law, but the court will not be required to follow it. Therefore, it is best to look for cases from your state or your federal appeals circuit.

FINDING CASE LAW

DIGESTS

Digests are the primary source for finding case law in reporters (described on page 44 in the section titled "Case Reporters"). This is because reporters are not indexed. The digest is a compilation of *abstracts*, or summaries, of cases in a particular jurisdiction or legal area. These abstracts, along with the topic and key number (discussed in the subsection on page 42 titled "Topic and Key Number"), are an integral part of the way legal research is conducted. When these abstracts are printed in a reporter they are called *headnotes*, which will be discussed fully in the section on reporters.

State, federal or decennial. Each jurisdiction, whether state or federal, has its own digest. There is one digest for New York, one for Texas, one for California, a combined digest for Virginia and West Virginia and so on. Each digest is approximately thirty or forty volumes, with the exception of the decennial digests which have substantially more volumes than either the individual state digests or the federal digests. Digests may also have more than one edition so be sure to use the latest edition.

Example: You would want to use *Florida Digest 2d* before looking in *Florida Digest*, since *Florida Digest* covers cases decided before 1935. You should always search for the newest possible cases.

Decennial digests (*decennials*) are sets of digests that cover all of the states and all federal jurisdictions as well. They are grouped in ten year periods, hence the name "decennial." Since the *9th Decennial Digest*, the decennials have grown at such a tremendous rate that each ten-year period has been broken down into two five-year periods, for example, *11th Decennial Digest, Part I.*

Just to give you an idea of the growth rate, which corresponds directly to the number of cases being heard at the appellate level, the following is the breakdown of the number of volumes in the 7th, 8th, 9th, and 10th decennial (which is still being printed):

7th Decennial Digest:	38 volumes
8th Decennial Digest:	50 volumes
9th Decennial Digest (Parts 1 & 2):	108 volumes
10th Decennial Digest (Part 1):	is up to volume 50 in 2001

If you research in the decennials, you treat each ten-year period as if it were a separate set of books, unless you are researching in the 9th and 10th decennials, where you would research each part separately. Additionally, the decennials are updated by a set of books called the *General Digest*, which is in the 10th series (13 volumes in 2002 and growing). Each individual volume of this set must be researched individually until a compilation index is published. This compilation is in the back of each tenth volume, (10th, 20th, 30th, etc.). You will still find General Digest's 10th series on the shelf. These correspond to the 11th Decennial Digest, Part I. When all the 11th Decennials, Part II are published, the General Digest, 10th series volumes will be discarded.

You are probably asking why anyone would want to search through the decennials since they appear to be so cumbersome. This is true. Unless you plan on doing an all-encompassing search of all jurisdictions, you can avoid researching in the decennials. Any cases you would find in them, you will also find in the individual state or federal digests, so they are usually used as a last effort.

Before beginning any search in a digest, you will benefit from browsing through a few volumes to see the layout of the books. (See Figure 7 on page 54.)

Accessing the digest system. You access the digests through an index, generally called the *Descriptive Word Index*. (See Figure 8 on page 55.) Follow the directions for using an index in Chapter 1. Remember to look up every possible relevant word or phrase you can think of. Do not get discouraged if you do not find any of them at first. Continue to think of different words or phrases until you find a listing. Remember to use the dictionary, thesaurus and *Words and Phrases*. When you find a listing that pertains to your topic, write down the information.

Topic and key number. You will find that a digest index does not refer you to a page. Instead, it refers you to a word, phrase, or abbreviation, which are in bold face type; and a number, for example "Divorce 238." This is called a *topic and key number*. There is a table in the front of each digest volume listing what each topic abbreviation represents. For example, "Evid" is an abbreviation for "Evidence," and "App & E" an abbreviation for "Appeal and Error."

The main volumes of the digest are set up alphabetically, like a standard encyclopedia, but instead of saying "Photography to Pumpkin," it will likely say "Pretrial Procedure to Records". When you go to the volume containing "Divorce," turn the pages until you see "Divorce" followed by the picture of a key and the number "238" in the upper right or upper left hand corner. It is this "Divorce 238" that is the topic and key number, "Divorce" being the topic and "238" being the key number. (See Figure 7 on page 54.)

Notice that the page is double-columned and is filled with small paragraphs. These paragraphs are abstracts, or summaries, of all the cases in that jurisdiction discussing that distinct point of law. Only that one element of the law will be considered under "Divorce 238," in this case the nature and right of permanent alimony. A different element of the law will be discussed under "Divorce 239." The digest system reduces each and every point to its own topic and key number.

NOTE: *When you discover a useful topic and key number in one jurisdiction, you can look up cases in any other jurisdiction as well. This is because digests using the key number system are published by one publisher, West Publishing Company, and the topic and key number system is uniform throughout the entire digest system.*

If you proceed to "Divorce 238" in another digest, you will notice that those case abstracts, although dealing with another state or court, discuss the exact same point of law.

Example: Assume you have been researching Florida law and "Divorce 238," permanent alimony, is pertinent to your research. You decide you'd like to see New York cases dealing with permanent alimony. All you need to do is look up "Divorce 238" in the digest for New York. The topic will be the same. Try it with Hawaii, Michigan, Texas, or any other state. You will see that the subject matter of "Divorce 238" is the same for each of those states as well.

READING A
CASE CITATION

Each case summary from the digest will give you the complete citation to the case to which it refers. A citation is the way all legal materials are quoted. It is a form of legal shorthand used to give information about where a case or statute can be found. When you have a citation you will already know a great deal of information about a case. A case citation looks like this:

Roth Greeting Cards v. United Card Co., 429 F.2d 1106 (9th Cir. 1970).

"*Roth Greeting Cards v. United Card Co.*" means Roth Greeting Cards versus United Card Co., in which Roth Greeting Cards is the party that brought the appeal (having lost in the trial court) and United Card Co. is the party defending against the appeal (having won in the trial court). The first-named party is always the party appealing the case.

"429" refers to volume 429. "F.2d" is an abbreviation of the reporter, in this instance Federal Reporter, 2nd Series. "1106" refers to page 1106, and "(1970)" refers to the year the case was decided.

Sometimes a case citation will give additional information as well, such as the abbreviation of the court that wrote the opinion, in this case the 9th Circuit Court of Appeals.

If the case summary seems relevant to your problem, write down the citation. Then you can look the case up in the reporter and read the full text of the opinion.

> *Warning:* Never argue a point of law based on a case abstract from a digest, statute annotation, or elsewhere. You must read the full text of the opinion to determine if the case really applies to your problem.

POCKET PARTS

Now is a good time to discuss pocket parts. A *pocket part* is a small pamphlet placed in a slat, or pocket, in the book. Usually the pocket is placed on the inside back cover, but is occasionally on the inside front cover. The pocket part is a supplement, or update, of the hardbound volume. Publishers use pocket parts to avoid reprinting the volume with each change in the law, which occurs frequently. It is essential to always look in the pocket part for new information if a set of books is updated with pocket parts. The information in the pocket part will be laid out in the identical manner to the main volume it is supplementing. Although not all books are updated in this manner, digests are, so if you are researching Divorce 238 you can look it up in the pocket part exactly as you did in the main volume.

CASE REPORTERS

As stated earlier, case reporters are sets of books in which court opinions are printed.

Opinions. A court *opinion* is the written decision of a court. Although the word "opinion" is used, do not confuse it with its common meaning. A court's opinion is much more than the judge's *belief* about a legal matter. A court's opinion is a formal statement explaining how the court applied the law to a particular set of circumstances to arrive at its determination of the case. It is *binding* on the parties concerned; that is, all parties involved in the case *must* comply with the court's decision or be subject to *contempt* of court. *Contempt of court*, meaning that a judge

believes that a participant in her courtroom was willfully disobedient or disrespectful to the judge, the court itself and/or the law, could include a monetary fine or jail.

As said before, in general only appellate court decisions are reported. (There are exceptions which will be discussed later in this chapter on page 48 under the subheading "Federal Cases.") Appellate court cases are customarily heard by a panel—a group of judges that is smaller than the entire court. For example, if an appellate court has nine judges total, it will probably be split into three panels of three judges each. This means that if a panel hears an appellate argument, three judges will listen to the argument. On occasion however, the full court may sit and provide an opinion.

The Supreme Court of the United States is an appellate court in which all nine justices sit and listen to arguments. When all of an appellate court's judges sit in on an argument it is called *en banc* which means "in the bench" or "full bench." Argument refers to the remarks or oral presentation made in court by attorneys on behalf of the parties involved.

Parts of an opinion. A court's opinion may consist of up to three parts, the majority, the dissent, and the concurrence.

1. *The majority opinion.* The *majority opinion* of an appellate court decision is one in which the majority of the court's members have joined and agreed. It is usually written by one judge and the other judges declare that they agree with his or her opinion. This means that if the panel listening to the argument has three judges, at least two judges must agree with each other for there to be a majority opinion. If nine judges are sitting on the panel, at least five must agree with each other for the opinion to be the majority opinion. The majority opinion is the opinion that the parties to the lawsuit must abide by. This is also the opinion that you will look to as precedent when you do research.

2. *The dissent.* The *dissent*, or dissenting or minority opinion, is a separate opinion in which one or more judges of a court expressly disagree with the majority. Very often the judge or judges disagreeing with the majority

will write an individual opinion explaining why he or she disagrees, although a judge may dissent without writing an explanation. The dissenting opinion does not set precedent.

NOTE: *If you discover while doing your research, that all you can find are cases which only have support for your position in the dissent or concurrence (discussed below), you will have to try to make a persuasive argument. It will not have the same weight that the precedent set in the majority opinion has, and in fact, will probably be ignored by most judges. This is usually an indication that your position is not very good.*

3. *The concurrence.* In a *concurrence,* or *concurring opinion,* a judge (or judges) agrees with the conclusion of the majority but disagrees with its reasoning.

Example: The majority opinion says that Smith shall recover money for injuries he received in a car accident with Jones and sets out all the legal rules and principles it followed to come to that conclusion. By concurring, a judge is saying: "I agree that Smith should recover the money for his injuries, but for different reasons than those legal rules and principles followed by the majority." Perhaps the majority states that Smith should prevail based on the theory of negligence, while the concurring judge thinks that he should prevail because of the theory of strict liability.

It is possible for the entire panel to disagree as to the legal rules and principles followed to come to a conclusion. All, or most, of the judges may write concurring opinions. When this happens the opinion is not called a majority since no consensus of the court has been reached. It is called a *plurality* instead.

In our previous example, Smith would still recover money for his injuries since the panel would agree to that result, but no clear precedent explaining why he prevailed would be set since the judges could not agree as to the legal reasons Smith should recover the money. Always look for a case in which clear precedent has been set.

Per curiam opinion. A *per curiam* opinion is not a part of an opinion. Meaning "by the court," it is one in which the entire court joins, but the name of the judge who wrote the opinion is not revealed, and as a rule, the opinion will state a result without giving a reason. Consequently, per curiam opinions are not given great weight.

The reporter system. The *reporter system* is a collection of opinions that are published in sets. Each volume of the set is numbered consecutively and each case in the volume is printed chronologically.

State cases. Most reporters are published by West Publishing Company. West publishes the cases in "regional reporters," which divide the country into regions. The regional reporters and the states they cover are displayed in Table 1 on page 58.

Most jurisdictions also have their own reporters. There are two types of these reporters, official and unofficial. It will suffice for you to know that official reporters are published by the state itself and that the unofficial reporters are generally published by West Publishing Co. Most states have discontinued publication of official reporters because it costs too much to publish and West does a good job of reporting. Whether you read a case in an official or an unofficial reporter is not important to your research. The case will read the same except for any editorial comment that West Publishing, or other reporting service, will prepare before the case. Also, because of the prohibitive cost of upkeep, most libraries do not stock the official reporters of other states.

NOTE: *When you look up a case in, say, Florida Cases (this is a special version of the Southern Reporter, 2d Series which only includes cases from Florida courts), you may notice that the book may skip between pages 5 and 60 or between pages 131 and 164—in other words the pages may not be consecutive. If you had looked up your case in the regional reporter, Southern Reporter, 2d Series, however, those pages would have been there. That is because pages 6 through 59 covered cases from another state that were published in that region. So there is no need to be nervous and think that the book is defective or that someone tore pages from the book.*

Federal cases. Publication of reporters for the federal system is a little easier to remember than the state reporter system because there are no regional reporters in the federal system. All federal reporters correspond to the court from which the cases come, regardless of their geographical area.

Example: A Court of Appeals case from Pennsylvania will be reported in *Federal Reporter*, as will a Court of Appeals case from California.

The federal system, which is separated into circuits, is described in Table 2 on page 59.

In general, there are only six sets of reporters in the federal reporter system. All courts of appeal cases are published in *Federal Reporter*, as stated above. All bankruptcy court cases are published in *Bankruptcy Reporter*, and certain federal cases concerning rules of procedure and evidence may be published in *Federal Rules Decisions*.

Although trial (i.e., district court) cases are not usually published, a few are printed in the *Federal Supplement*. This is the exception to the general rule stated above that only appellate cases are reported. The judge who hears the case determines if the case will be published, and in general, only one to ten percent of federal district court cases are printed.

Cases that pre-date 1880 are printed in *Federal Cases*. With the exception of *Federal Cases*, which compiles cases reported from 1789–1879 and is arranged alphabetically, all reporters are compiled chronologically, like the state reporters. All of these sets of books are published by West Publishing Company.

United States Supreme Court cases are published in three separate reporters, published by three different publishers. All Supreme Court cases will be found in each set of books.

The first is an official reporter published by the United States Government Printing Office (GPO). In it cases are printed without any editorial comment. This set of books is usually six to nine months behind in publication. It is called *United States Reports* and is abbreviated "U.S."

The second is published by West Publishing and is called *Supreme Court Reporter*, abbreviated "S.Ct." The editorial commentary is identical to that of every other reporter in the West reporter system, which as you can see by now, encompasses most of the reporters—state and federal. This editorial commentary will be described in full detail on page __.

The third set of books that compiles the United States Supreme Court decisions is *United States Reports, Lawyers Edition*, abbreviated "L.Ed." or "L.Ed. 2d", known as "Lawyers Edition." This should not be confused with the *United States Reports* published by the GPO. In addition to any commentary before the actual case is reported, *Lawyers Edition* has the *briefs* (a written outline of the attorneys' arguments) written by the attorneys, and any *amicus curae* (which means "friends of the court") in a section in the back of each volume. The briefs may help you see how legal arguments are made to a court.

Headnotes in a case reporter. One of the most important aspects of a case in the West system is the *headnote*, which was briefly discussed in the section on "digests" on page 40. Headnotes precede the actual printed opinion in the reporter. A headnote is a brief summary of a legal rule or significant fact in a case. In a digest this would be the abstract of a case. The headnote is important to legal research, because once you find a headnote that is important you can go back to the digest and find additional cases covering that topic.

Study Figure 9 on pages 56 and 57, which are copies of the first two pages of a case reported in volume 658, of the *Pacific Reporter, 2d Series*. Notice that after the syllabus, or summary of the case, there are a series of numbers, 1 through 10, followed by topics and key numbers, and then case abstracts. The numbers, 1-10, and the abstracts are called the headnotes. Technically, the topic and key number are not part of the headnote, but most people consider the entire paragraph to be the headnote.

Now, assume that you find this case in the digest for Alaska when you determine that the topic and key number "Indians 24" may be important to your research. As you glance at the headnotes however, you

notice that "**Indians 27(1)**" is also very important. You can return to the digest, look up "**Indians 27(1)**," and find additional cases related to your problem. But remember that just as you cannot use the digest abstracts as the sole basis for your research, neither can you use headnotes in that fashion. Unless the headnote is taken verbatim from the text of the opinion, you may never quote a headnote in any court document.

Another interesting editorial aspect of headnotes is that the number of the headnote makes it easy to find that point of law or fact in the case itself. You may have a case that is ten, twenty, or even fifty pages long. What if only headnote 5 applies to your problem? How would you find that point of law without reading through the entire case? Notice in Figure 9 that immediately after "II. DISCUSSION" there is a "[1]". This bracketed number refers to headnote number 1. The point of law or facts corresponding to headnote 1 will be discussed in that section of the opinion. This is an especially handy tool when your case is long and has many headnotes.

Headnotes are also helpful when you are using *Shepard's Citations*, which will be discussed in detail in Chapter 5.

Other editorial comment. As was stated before, the syllabus is a summary of the case being reported. This syllabus is not part of the case. Neither are the headnotes. This is because neither the syllabus nor the headnotes were written by the court. These were added by the publisher to help you save time in your research. Look at Figure 9 once more. After the headnote numbered 10 there is a short horizontal line. All the material *after* that line is the actual case opinion, and may be quoted as legally significant since it was written by the court.

Incidentally, the citation for the case shown in Figure 9 is: *Native Village of Eyak v. GC Contractors*, 658 P.2d 756 (Alaska 1983).

ADVANCE SHEETS

Not all sets of legal books are updated with pocket parts. Case reporters are numbered consecutively and the opinions are printed in chronological order. Any supplementation required must *follow* the last case in the set. For this reason reporters are updated by use of *advance sheets* which add

new case opinions to the set, instead of with pocket parts, which supplement existing materials. Advance sheets are not really "sheets," as in separate sheets of paper, but are pamphlets. Unlike pocket parts, they have a cover and are placed at the end of the last volume in the set of reporters instead of being placed inside the volumes. The cases are laid out exactly as they are in the hardbound reporter volumes.

There may be as many as twenty advance sheets on the library shelf for each set of reporters but that should not worry you. Each advance sheet is numbered in a fashion corresponding to the reporter series so when a suitable number of cases have been printed in the advance sheets, the publisher will print a hardbound edition, and the advance sheets for that volume will be discarded. For example, if the last hardbound volume in the reporter series *Pacific Reporter, 3rd Series* (P.3d) is number 32, pages 1073 to1294; Volume 33, pages 1 to 183 and so forth until there are enough pamphlets to print a hardbound Volume 33. When a hardbound Volume 33 is released, the advance sheets corresponding to Volume 33 will be discarded.

LOOSELEAF
SERVICES

Looseleaf services, sometimes just called *looseleafs*, are just what the name suggests, looseleaf binders. These sets of books may be one volume but are usually multiple volumes. Looseleafs are used for many different types of legal materials, but case reporting is one of their major uses. Looseleaf services are always published by private companies.

The main advantage of looseleaf services, and the reason many legal practitioners use them and buy subscriptions to them, is that looseleaf publishers print new cases and other legal materials much faster than the materials printed in reporters. Since the materials are just inserted into looseleaf binders, they do not require binding, which can extend printing time significantly.

Up until just five or six years ago, the time difference between the first printing in a looseleaf and the printing in a reporter advance sheet could have been three to four weeks or more. Today, the lag is not as acute for those with access to computerized databases (see Chapter 7), but it is

still at least two weeks without computer access. This time difference could be very important in some instances, especially when a new case affects the potential outcome of a client's problem.

Occasionally, there are cases that are not even printed in a reporter. Some looseleaf services print these cases. Remember, the case has to be printed before it is considered precedent.

Looseleafs are generally easy to use. They either are updated by inserting new materials behind previously printed ones, or by removing old pages and inserting new ones in their place. This is a tedious process, which does not affect the user since it is done by the library staff. The one significant downside to looseleaf services is that, until the material is printed in a reporter system, the cases are not considered "official" and may be changed or even withdrawn. Only cite to a case in a looseleaf if you cannot find it in a reporter, either because it is not printed in a reporter yet or it is the type of case that is not printed in a reporter at all.

Figure 6: The State and Federal Court System

THE STATE COURT SYSTEM

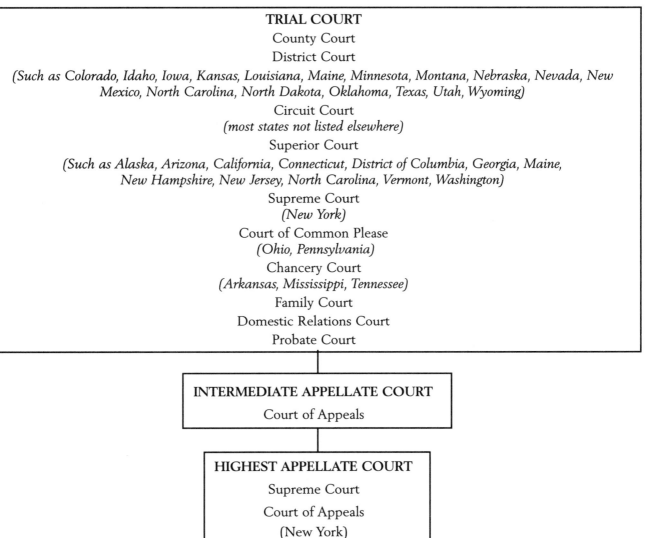

TRIAL COURT

County Court

District Court

(Such as Colorado, Idaho, Iowa, Kansas, Louisiana, Maine, Minnesota, Montana, Nebraska, Nevada, New Mexico, North Carolina, North Dakota, Oklahoma, Texas, Utah, Wyoming)

Circuit Court

(most states not listed elsewhere)

Superior Court

(Such as Alaska, Arizona, California, Connecticut, District of Columbia, Georgia, Maine, New Hampshire, New Jersey, North Carolina, Vermont, Washington)

Supreme Court

(New York)

Court of Common Please

(Ohio, Pennsylvania)

Chancery Court

(Arkansas, Mississippi, Tennessee)

Family Court

Domestic Relations Court

Probate Court

INTERMEDIATE APPELLATE COURT

Court of Appeals

HIGHEST APPELLATE COURT

Supreme Court

Court of Appeals

(New York)

THE FEDERAL COURT SYSTEM

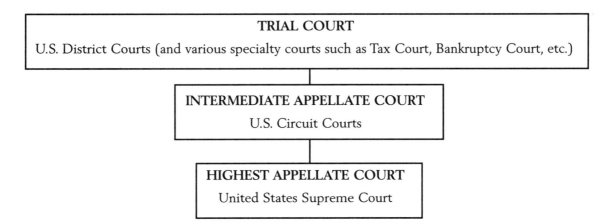

TRIAL COURT

U.S. District Courts (and various specialty courts such as Tax Court, Bankruptcy Court, etc.)

INTERMEDIATE APPELLATE COURT

U.S. Circuit Courts

HIGHEST APPELLATE COURT

United States Supreme Court

For reference to other topics, see Descriptive-Word Index

Va.App. 1988. Mere facts that marriage was of short duration and wife maintained her net worth throughout marriage were insufficient to support decision to deny spousal support to wife; court was required to consider both parties' reasonable needs and abilities to provide support.

Keyser v. Keyser, 374 S.E.2d 698, 7 Va. App. 405.

Va.App. 1988. Fault in dissolution of marriage represents only one factor and should not be used to punish economically either party. Code 1950, § 20–107.3.

Aster v. Gross, 371 S.E.2d 833, 7 Va.App. 1.

Va.App. 1987. Right to spousal support is not affected by award of no-fault divorce since neither party's duty of support is affected absent finding of "fault," i.e., grounds which legally may be used by one party as basis for obtaining divorce, on one party or the other.

Surbey v. Surbey, 360 S.E.2d 873, 5 Va. App. 119.

Wife's adulterous conduct after separation did not bar her claim for spousal support in light of evidence that husband also committed adultery during that time; only existing ground for divorce was separation without cohabitation for more than one year. Code 1950, § 20–91(9)(c).

Surbey v. Surbey, 360 S.E.2d 873, 5 Va. App. 119.

Va.App. 1986. Wife was not entitled to spousal support when husband established grounds for divorce based upon desertion, even though trial court had granted divorce under one-year separation statute. Code 1950, §§ 20–91(6), 20–107.1.

Zinkhan v. Zinkhan, 342 S.E.2d 658, 2 Va.App. 200.

Va.App. 1986. Award of no-fault divorce to one spouse does not affect right of the spouse to spousal support. Code 1950, §§ 20–91(9), 20–107.1.

Dukelow v. Dukelow, 341 S.E.2d 208, 2 Va.App. 21.

Va.App. 1986. Wife had no right to spousal support where divorce was granted to husband because of wife's desertion. Code 1950, § 20–107.1.

D'Auria v. D'Auria, 340 S.E.2d 164, 1 Va. App. 455.

Va.App. 1986. Where evidence supported chancellor's finding that husband was entitled to a divorce on the grounds of desertion, wife was not entitled to support and maintenance.

Rexrode v. Rexrode, 339 S.E.2d 544, 1 Va.App. 385.

Va.App. 1985. Wife was not barred from receiving spousal support where husband alleged she had committed adultery 15 years after parties separated but evidence showed that the husband was responsible for termination of marriage. Code 1950, § 20–107.1.

Wallace v. Wallace, 336 S.E.2d 27, 1 Va. App. 183.

W.Va. 1998. Trial court abused its discretion in making an award of rehabilitative alimony in lieu of permanent alimony upon termination of 27–year marriage, even though ex-wife received a significant cash award from ex-husband's 401k plan, where ex-wife's wages as a cashier were approximately $12,000, ex-husband's wages as a business executive were in excess of $100,000, there was nothing in the record to establish that ex-wife's potential wages as a cashier would ever approach those earned by ex-husband, and ex-husband also retained marital assets.

Ward v. Ward, 504 S.E.2d 917, 202 W.Va. 454.

W.Va. 1997. Condonation defense did not apply in context of alimony determination.

Hastings v. Hastings, 497 S.E.2d 203, 201 W.Va. 354.

Alimony is barred, where prospective recipient has committed adultery, where, subsequent to the marriage, prospective recipient has been convicted of a felony and conviction is final, and where prospective recipient has actually abandoned or deserted the other spouse for six months; in other situations, court or family law master shall consider and compare spouses' fault or misconduct and the effect of such fault or misconduct as a contributing factor to the deterioration of the marital relationship. Code, 48–2–15(i).

Hastings v. Hastings, 497 S.E.2d 203, 201 W.Va. 354.

W.Va. 1997. Alimony must not be disproportionate to person's ability to pay as disclosed by evidence before court.

Pearson v. Pearson, 488 S.E.2d 414, 200 W.Va. 139.

Fault premium for maintenance/alimony award may be applied to discourage fault or behavior that contributed to dissolution of marriage.

Pearson v. Pearson, 488 S.E.2d 414, 200 W.Va. 139.

In determining award of maintenance/alimony enhanced by fault premium, circuit court must consider concrete financial realities of parties.

Pearson v. Pearson, 488 S.E.2d 414, 200 W.Va. 139.

References are to Digest Topics and Key Numbers

ALIMONY—Cont'd

COMPROMISE, Compromise ☞ 3

CONCLUSIVENESS of adjudication, **Divorce** ☞ 255

CONFLICT of laws, **Divorce** ☞ 199.5(1-3)

CONSTITUTIONAL and statutory provisions, **Divorce** ☞ 199.7(1-10)
  Purpose, **Divorce** ☞ 199.7(2)
  Retroactive operation, **Divorce** ☞ 199.7(8-10)
  Validity, **Divorce** ☞ 199.7(4-6)

CONTEMPT for failure to pay, **Divorce** ☞ 269
  Foreign alimony decree, **Divorce** ☞ 397(3)

CONTRACTS, **Divorce** ☞ 236

CONVEYANCES,
  Fraud of spouse's right to alimony, **Divorce** ☞ 275, 276
  Property awarded, **Divorce** ☞ 259

COSTS, **Divorce** ☞ 288

DEATH of party as terminating, **Divorce** ☞ 247

DECISIONS reviewable, **Divorce** ☞ 280

DECREE. See subheading JUDGMENT or decree under this heading.

DECRETAL judgment, **Divorce** ☞ 277

DEFENSES and objections to award of,
  Attorney fees and expenses, **Divorce** ☞ 225
  Permanent alimony, **Divorce** ☞ 238
  Temporary alimony, **Divorce** ☞ 213

DELIVERY of property awarded, **Divorce** ☞ 259

DETERMINATION and disposition of questions on appeal, **Divorce** ☞ 287

DISCRETION of court,
  Attorney fees and expenses, **Divorce** ☞ 223
  Permanent alimony, **Divorce** ☞ 235
  Review, **Divorce** ☞ 286(3)
  Temporary alimony, **Divorce** ☞ 211
    Review, **Divorce** ☞ 286(4)

DISPOSITION of property, **Divorce** ☞ 248.1-254(2)
  Generally, **Divorce** ☞ 248.1
  Agreement of parties, **Divorce** ☞ 249.2
  Appeal, **Divorce** ☞ 278-287
  Application and proceedings thereon, **Divorce** ☞ 253
  Award of specific property, **Divorce** ☞ 242
  Child custody, effect on disposition of residence, **Divorce** ☞ 252.5(2)

ALIMONY—Cont'd
DISPOSITION of property—Cont'd

  Community property, **Divorce** ☞ 252.3(2)
  Compensating payments, **Divorce** ☞ 252.3(5)
  Conflict of laws, **Divorce** ☞ 199.5(3)
  Creditors' rights, **Divorce** ☞ 252.4
  Debts and liabilities, **Divorce** ☞ 252.4
  Delivery or conveyance of property awarded, **Divorce** ☞ 259
  Discretion of court, **Divorce** ☞ 252.1
  Discretion of court, review, **Divorce** ☞ 286(5)
  Evidence, **Divorce** ☞ 253(2)
  Fact questions, review, **Divorce** ☞ 286(8)
  Foreign divorces, **Divorce** ☞ 399
  Homestead, **Divorce** ☞ 252.5(1-3)
  Injunction against disposition before award, **Divorce** ☞ 206
  Insurance rights, **Divorce** ☞ 252.3(4)
  Joint property, **Divorce** ☞ 252.3(2)
  Judgment or decree, **Divorce** ☞ 254; **Divorce** ☞ 254(1, 2)
  Mode of allocation, **Divorce** ☞ 252.3(1-5)
  Modification, judgment or decree, **Divorce** ☞ 254(2)
  Particular property, **Divorce** ☞ 252.3(1-5)
  Pension rights, **Divorce** ☞ 252.3(4)
  Power and authority of court, **Divorce** ☞ 249.1
  Premarital property, **Divorce** ☞ 252.3(3)
  Proceedings, **Divorce** ☞ 253(1-4)
  Professional degrees and licenses, **Divorce** ☞ 252.3(1)
  Proportion or share given on division, **Divorce** ☞ 252.2
  Residence, **Divorce** ☞ 252.5(1-3)
  Retirement rights, **Divorce** ☞ 252.3(4)
  Retroactive operation of statutes, **Divorce** ☞ 199.7(10)
  Sale or distribution in kind, **Divorce** ☞ 252.3(5)
  Separate property, **Divorce** ☞ 252.3(3)
  Stage of proceedings, **Divorce** ☞ 249.7
  Stipulations of parties, **Divorce** ☞ 249.2
  Vacation, judgment or decree, **Divorce** ☞ 254(2)
  Validity of statutes, **Divorce** ☞ 199.7(6)
  Valuation of assets, **Divorce** ☞ 253(3)
  Verdict or findings, **Divorce** ☞ 253(4)
  Waste, **Divorce** ☞ 252.3(1)

DISTRIBUTION of property,
  Consortium claims, **Divorce** ☞ 252.3(1)
  Contingency fees, **Divorce** ☞ 252.3(1)
  Equitable distribution, **Divorce** ☞ 252.3(1)

NATIVE VILLAGE OF EYAK,
Appellant,

v.

GC CONTRACTORS, Appellee.

No. 6274.

Supreme Court of Alaska.

Jan. 14, 1983.

Suit was instituted by a native village to foreclose on a lien recorded by the contractor. The Superior Court, Third Judicial District, Milton M. Souter, J., entered judgment confirming an arbitration award in favor of contractor and rejected affirmative defense of immunity from suit, and native village appealed. The Supreme Court, Compton, J., held that: (1) the native village against which contractor sought to foreclose on a lien filed in connection with contract to build a community center for village was not immune from suit even if it was a federally recognized tribal entity since it agreed to submit to arbitration any disputes arising from the contract and thus waived whatever immunity it possessed; (2) the native village could waive tribal sovereign immunity without obtaining congressional authorization; (3) contract containing arbitration clause was not illegal because not approved by the Secretary of the Interior; and (4) arbitration clause was a sufficiently clear and unequivocal waiver of immunity to be effective.

Affirmed.

1. Indians ⬥27(1)

One of the sovereign privileges that Indian tribes possess is immunity from suit.

2. Indians ⬥27(1)

The native village against which contractor sought to foreclose on a lien filed in connection with contract to build a community center for village was not immune from suit even if it was a federally recognized tribal entity since it agreed to submit to arbitration any disputes arising from the contract and thus waived whatever immunity it possessed.

3. Appeal and Error ⬥854(1), 856(1)

The Supreme Court may affirm a judgment of the superior court on different grounds than those advanced by the superior court and even on grounds not raised by the parties in the superior court.

4. Indians ⬥27(1)

The phrase "without congressional authorization," within rule exempting all Indian nations from suit without congressional authorization, cannot be construed to mean that an Indian tribe is unable to waive its immunity.

5. Indians ⬥27(1)

An Indian tribe may waive its sovereign immunity without obtaining congressional authorization.

6. Indians ⬥24

Statute requiring the Secretary of the Interior to approve all contracts made by Indian tribes that relate to their tribal land or to claims against the United States was not applicable to contract between native village and contractor, even assuming native village was an Indian tribe, where contract involved construction of a community center on property leased from a third party and did not involve tribal land. 25 U.S.C.A. § 81.

7. Arbitration ⬥7.4

Any dispute arising from a contract cannot be resolved by arbitration, as specified in contract, if one of the parties intends to assert the defense of sovereign immunity.

8. Contracts ⬥143.5

To the extent possible, all provisions in a contract should be found meaningful.

9. Indians ⬥27(1)

A clause in a contract stating that the federal courts will resolve any disputes arising from the contract constitutes an express waiver of an Indian tribe's sovereign immunity and, with respect to an agreement that any dispute arising from a contract shall be resolved by the federal courts and an agree-

NATIVE VILLAGE OF EYAK v. GC CONTRACTORS Alaska **757**
Cite as, 658 P.2d 756 (Alaska 1983)

ment that any dispute shall be resolved by arbitration, there is little substantive difference, and both appear to be clear indications that sovereign immunity has been waived.

10. Indians ☞27(1)

Arbitration clause which was contained in contract calling for contractor to build a community center for a native village and which provided that disputes arising under the contract were to be resolved by arbitration amounted to an effective waiver of whatever immunity from suit the native village may have possessed.

Roger L. Hudson, Roberts & Shefelman, Anchorage, for appellant.

Kenneth O. Jarvi, Law Offices of Kenneth O. Jarvi, Anchorage, for appellee.

Robert E. Price, Asst. Atty. Gen., Wilson L. Condon, Atty. Gen., Juneau, for amicus curiae State of Alaska.

Before BURKE, C.J., RABINOWITZ and COMPTON, JJ., and DIMOND, Senior Justice.*

OPINION

COMPTON, Justice.

In this appeal, the Native Village of Eyak ("Eyak") contends that it is an "Indian tribe" and therefore immune from the suit brought against it by appellee GC Contractors. Eyak further contends that it did not waive its immunity by entering into a contract with GC Contractors containing an arbitration clause. We disagree with this contention. For the reasons set forth below, we conclude that it is not necessary to determine whether Eyak is an Indian tribe because, assuming that it is, Eyak waived whatever immunity it possessed when it agreed to resolve by arbitration any disputes that arose under its contract with GC Contractors.

* Dimond, Senior Justice, sitting by assignment made pursuant to article IV, section 16, of the

I. FACTUAL AND PROCEDURAL BACKGROUND

In 1977, Eyak entered into a contract with GC Contractors, Inc., under which GC Contractors was to build a community center for Eyak on land leased by Eyak. The contract provided that disputes arising under it were to be resolved by arbitration. Eyak received a grant from the United States Economic Development Administration to pay for its community center.

Although GC Contractors completed construction of the community center, Eyak failed to pay $13,745.98 due under the contract. GC Contractors sued Eyak in the superior court to foreclose on a lien it had recorded. Eyak answered the complaint, denying it owed the money. It also asserted as affirmative defenses that it was immune from suit and that the parties had agreed by contract to submit disputes to arbitration. GC Contractors noticed the matter for arbitration and proceedings were subsequently held. Eyak again contended that it was immune from suit and argued that it would not be bound by the arbitration decision. The arbitrator impliedly rejected this argument and awarded GC Contractors the full sum sought.

GC Contractors requested confirmation of the award in the superior court. The court ruled that Eyak failed to establish that it is an Indian tribe and the court accordingly confirmed the arbitration award. Eyak appeals from this determination.

II. DISCUSSION

[1] Eyak's principal argument on appeal is that the superior court erred in ruling that it is not an Indian tribe. Indian tribes have been held to possess many but not all of the privileges of sovereignty that foreign nations and the United States hold. *E.g., White Mountain Apache Tribe v. Bracker*, 448 U.S. 136, 142, 100 S.Ct. 2578, 2583, 65 L.Ed.2d 665, 671 (1980); *Santa Clara Pueblo v. Martinez*, 436 U.S. 49, 58, 98 S.Ct. 1670, 1677, 56 L.Ed.2d 106, 115 (1978); *United States v. Wheeler*, 435 U.S. 313, 322–26, 98

Constitution of Alaska and Alaska R.Admin.P. 23(a).

Table 1: Regional Reporters

A. and A.2d	Atlantic Reporter	Connecticut, Delaware, District of Columbia, Maine, Maryland, New Hampshire, New Jersey, Pennsylvania, Rhode Island, Vermont.
Cal. Rptr. and Cal. Rptr.2d	California Reporter	California
N.E. and N.E.2d	Northeastern Reporter	Illinois, Indiana, Massachusetts, New York, Ohio; also New York Court of Appeals.
N.Y.S.	New York Supplement	New York.
N.W. and N.W.2d	Northwestern Reporter	Iowa, Michigan, Minnesota, Nebraska, North Dakota, South Dakota, Wisconsin.
P., P.2d, and P.3d	Pacific Reporter	Alaska, Arizona, California Supreme Court since 1960, Colorado, Hawaii, Idaho, Kansas, Montana, Nevada, New Mexico, Oklahoma, Oregon, Utah, Washington, Wyoming.
S.E. and S.E.2d	Southeastern Reporter	Georgia, North Carolina, South Carolina, Virginia, West Virginia.
So. and So.2d	Southern Reporter	Alabama, Florida, Louisiana, Mississippi.
S.W,. S.W.2d, and S.W.3d	Southwestern Reporter	Arkansas, Kentucky, Missouri, Tennessee, Texas.

Table 2: Courts of Appeal Circuits

Circuit Number/Name	Jurisdiction Covered/Location
1st	Maine, New Hampshire, Rhode Island, Massachusetts, Puerto Rico Location: Boston, MA
2nd	New York, Vermont, Connecticut Location: New York, NY
3rd	Pennsylvania, New Jersey, Delaware, Virgin Islands Location: Philadelphia, PA
4th	West Virginia, Virginia, Maryland, North Carolina, South Carolina Location: Richmond, VA
5th	Louisiana, Texas, Mississippi, Canal Zone (until given back to Panama) Location: New Orleans, LA
6th	Michigan, Ohio, Kentucky, Tennessee Location: Cincinnati, OH
7th	Wisconsin, Illinois, Indiana Location: Chicago, IL
8th	Minnesota, Iowa, Missouri, Arkansas, Nebraska, South Dakota, North Dakota Location: St. Louis, MO
9th	Hawaii, Washington, Oregon, Idaho, Montana, Nevada, Arizona, California, Alaska, Guam, N. Mariana Islands; Location: San Francisco, CA

Circuit Number/Name	Jurisdiction Covered/Location
10th	Wyoming, Colorado, Utah, New Mexico, Kansas, Oklahoma Location: Denver, CO
11th	Alabama, Florida, Georgia (before October 1, 1981, this was part of the 5th circuit) Location: Atlanta, GA
District of Columbia	Washington, D.C.
Federal Circuit	Patent and Customs cases Location: Washington, DC

SHEPARD'S CITATIONS 5

As was discussed earlier, American jurisprudence is largely based on case law. Lawyers and judges look to *precedent* to determine what the law is, or is not, when a problem is presented to them. Precedent is a prior court decision that sets the example of the rule of law for the current decision. Like lawyers and judges, you have now done some case research and hopefully have found many cases that support your situation. Yet how can you be sure that these cases are "good law"? How do you know that these cases have not been overruled or reversed? The answer is a set of books called *Shepard's Citations*.

SHEPARD'S CITATIONS DEFINED

Shepard's, published by Shepard's/McGraw-Hill, is really nothing more than an index. When you look up a promising case in *Shepard's* you are led to each and every case that ever mentioned that case.

You have probably already read a few case opinions and noticed that judges cite other cases to support their arguments. *Shepard's* makes note of each case that is cited for any reason. *Shepard's* tells you if a case is overruled, reversed, explained, affirmed, or distinguished by these other cases. (See Figure 10 on page 67.) Remember, a case will only be of value to you if it is still valid. Neglecting to use *Shepard's* could leave

you with a position that is no longer of any legal significance. When you use *Shepard's* you are never in doubt as to whether a case is still "good law." This makes *Shepard's* an invaluable and necessary tool in legal research. You must master the art of *sheparsizing* if you want to do effective case research.

WHICH SHEPARD'S TO USE

When you first glance inside the cover of a *Shepard's Citations* you are likely to wince. It looks like hieroglyphics to the untrained eye. Do not let your initial reaction scare you. Once you understand what each column of numbers and letters is and how it works, using *Shepard's* really is very, very easy.

A separate *Shepard's* is printed for each reporter. So if you are shepardizing 271 So.2d 1, a Florida case, you would choose the *Shepard's* for *Southern Reporter* or for *Southern Reporter, Florida Cases* (if available in your library). Collect all of the volumes for that *Shepard's*. Each library places their *Shepard's* in different places. Some place the *Shepard's* directly after the reporter series it supports. Others have all the *Shepard's* in one place.

Shepard's usually consists of maroon-colored hardbound volumes and at least one yellow-colored paper pamphlet. In addition, there may be a red-colored paper pamphlet, a plain paper pamphlet (the cover is paper-colored), and a blue-covered *Shepard's Express*. Take all the *Shepard's* volumes for that reporter and place them in chronological order.

How do you know you have all the proper volumes? *Shepard's* makes it easy. The newest paper pamphlet, whether yellow, red or plain, always has a box on the front cover that says "WHAT YOUR LIBRARY SHOULD CONTAIN." This will tell you exactly what that *Shepard's* set includes. (See Figure 11 on page 68.) Any other volumes or pamphlets will be extraneous and should not be used. This may be especially true of libraries that neglect to discard outdated paper pamphlets. Just follow the directions on the cover and you will not be mislead.

How to Shepardize a Case

Once you have the *Shepard's* volumes in chronological order you are ready to shepardize your case. Remember, for our example we are shepardizing 272 So.2d 1 (called the *cited case*).

Realize that not all of *Shepard's* volumes will be helpful. One volume includes citations for *Southern Reporter, First Series* only. You will want to set aside that volume or any other that does not include your reporter volume. For example, if you are shepardizing a fairly new case you may find that only the pamphlets include that case's reporter volume. You would set aside all of the hardbound volumes in that instance. When you shepardize, you always begin with the newest *Shepard's* volume, usually a paper pamphlet, and work backwards. This insures that you are always finding the newest opinions that discuss the case you are interested in.

Now look at Figure 12 on page 69, illustrating a page from *Shepard's Citations* for *Southern Reporter, 2d Series (Florida Cases)*. Notice that the volume number, 272, is in bold print. In *Shepard's*, the page number from the reporter is distinguished by dashes on either side of the number, in this case -1-. This is how you find the exact volume and page of the case you are sheardizing. All of the case citations following are other case opinions in which your case was cited. Newer volumes of *Shepard's* print the case name for easier identification.

First, you will want to look in the space before the citations. Do you see an 'r,' 'd,' 'f,' or any other abbreviation that indicates case history or treatment? For example 271 So.2d 217 has cases with an 'f,' meaning "followed." This means that at 719 So.2d 328 (the *citing case*), the court followed the opinion as set out in the case, 271 So.2d 217 (again, called the cited case).

When you turn to page 328 of volume 719, you will immediately notice that you are in the middle of a case. Do not panic. You did not make a mistake. *Shepard's* brings you to the exact page where your case was

cited. This is especially handy when the citing case is many pages long. You may not want to read the entire case to determine if it's really helpful. This allows you to look at the exact context in which your case was discussed. Once you determine that the case may be helpful, you will want to read the entire case to make sure it is going to aid your situation.

Now that you have checked one case, you may want to look at the other cases to determine if they also are helpful. Yet how do you decide which cases are better, particularly when you are relying on a popularly cited case? *Shepard's* may have hundreds of citations listed.

Look at Figure 12 again. Notice the superscribed numbers printed between the reporter abbreviation and the page number. This number refers to the headnote. Our illustration shows that 708 So.2d 681 specifically refers to headnote 4. The '4' refers to headnote 4 in 272 So.2d 1, your original case. If this headnote was especially helpful to your situation you would look for any case in *Shepard's* making specific reference to that headnote. As you can see from Figure 12, other headnotes that were isolated were numbers 1, 2 and 5.

NOTE: *The blue-covered pamphlets called Shepard's Express are relatively new to the Shepard's family, and many older practitioners may not be very familiar with them. In an effort to get this information to you earlier (as much as three months), Shepard's notes whenever a case is cited but has not yet determined whether the citing case is overruling, distinguishing, reversing, affirming, etc.*

If you find your case is cited in one of these cases, you will have to read the entire case and determine whether your case has been affected by the citing case.

How to Shepardize a Statute

Shepardizing a statute follows the same basic rules as shepardizing a case. You obtain all the *Shepard's* volumes for your jurisdiction and separate the hardbound volumes pertaining to statutes and codes. You will also need the pamphlets (yellow and/or red) as well. Statute information is toward the back of the pamphlet.

It is understandable why you would shepardize a case. Finding other cases in *Shepard's* gives you a chain of cases that are all interrelated. It is not immediately clear why you would shepardize a statute or code, but it is important to do so.

When you look up a statute or code in *Shepard's* what you see first is legislative information about the statute. Has the statute been amended ("A"), added ("Ad"), or repealed (R)? *Shepard's* tells you (with the notations "A," "Ad," or "R"), along with the date of the change and where to locate the information in the session laws. (See Figures 13 and 14 on pages 72 and 73.) This will tell you at a glance whether or not the statute you are depending on is reliable.

After the legislative information, *Shepard's* cites to all cases that have construed or mentioned the statute. It will also tell you if a case has overruled the statute. In addition, *Shepard's* breaks down the statute into subdivisions. What this means is that if the portion of a statute applicable to your problem is 34.26(1)(a), you can shepardize for cases that construe not only 34.26, but 34.26(1) and 34.26(1)(a) specifically. This is important. Not only will you have a valid statute, you will have cases that are directly applicable to your situation. This information is at your fingertips without having to peruse pages and pages of statute annotations.

OTHER SHEPARD'S APPLICATIONS

Shepard's may be used for other sources as well. When you are shepardizing cases or statutes, you may find law review or A.L.R. (see Chapter 6) citations. Additionally, both law reviews and A.L.R.'s have *Shepard's* of their own. The methodology is identical to shepardizing a case.

ABBREVIATIONS—ANALYSIS

History of Case

a	(affirmed)	Same case affirmed on appeal.
cc	(connected case)	Different case from case cited but arising out of same subject matter or intimately connected therewith.
D	(dismissed)	Appeal from same case dismissed.
m	(modified)	Same case modified on appeal.
r	(reversed)	Same case reversed on appeal.
s	(same case)	Same case as case cited.
S	(superseded)	Substitution for former opinion.
v	(vacated)	Same case vacated.
US	cert den	Certiorari denied by U.S. Supreme Court.
US	cert dis	Certiorari dismissed by U.S. Supreme Court.
US	reh den	Rehearing denied by U.S. Supreme Court.
US	reh dis	Rehearing dismissed by U.S. Supreme Court.

Treatment of Case

c	(criticised)	Soundness of decision or reasoning in cited case criticised for reasons given.
d	(distinguished)	Case at bar different either in law or fact from case cited for reasons given.
e	(explained)	Statement of import of decision in cited case. Not merely a restatement of the facts.
f	(followed)	Cited as controlling.
h	(harmonized)	Apparent inconsistency explained and shown not to exist.
j	(dissenting opinion)	Citation in dissenting opinion.
L	(limited)	Refusal to extend decision of cited case beyond precise issues involved.
o	(overruled)	Ruling in cited case expressly overruled.
p	(parallel)	Citing case substantially alike or on all fours with cited case in its law or facts.
q	(questioned)	Soundness of decision or reasoning in cited case questioned.

ABBREVIATIONS—COURTS

Cir. DC–U.S. Court of Appeals, District of Columbia Circuit
Cir (number)–U.S. Court of Appeals Circuit (number)
Cir. Fed.–U.S. Court of Appeals, Federal Circuit
CCPA–Court of Customs and Patent Appeals
CIT–United States Court of International Trade
ClCt–Claims Court (U.S.)
CtCl–Court of Claims (U.S.)
CuCt–Customs Court
ECA–Temporary Emergency Court of Appeals
ML–Judicial Panel on Multidistrict Litigation
RRR–Special Court Regional Rail Reorganization Act of 1973

SHEPARD'S FLORIDA CITATIONS

Cumulative Supplement

WHAT YOUR LIBRARY SHOULD CONTAIN

1993 Bound Volumes, Cases (Parts 1-5)

1993 Bound Volumes, Statutes (Parts 1 and 2)

1993 –2001 Bound Supplement, Cases and Statutes,
   (Parts 1–3)*

Supplemented with:

–January 2002 Cumulative Supplement, Vol. 88 No. 1

DISCARD ALL OTHER ISSUES

Vol. 270 — SOUTHERN REPORTER, 2d SERIES (Florida Cases)

22FLW(D)
[2610
23FLW(D)251
Cir. 11
936FS[8]914

—770—
Lynch v McGovern
1972
723So2d274
731So2d[2]706
756So2d145
23FLW(D)
[1384
24FLW(D)330

Vol. 271

—1—
Hill v Douglass
1972
622So2d558

—7—
Belcher v Belcher
1972
620So2d1295
674So2d[3]930
674So2d[6]930
e 674So2d931
706So2d906
706So2d[3]907
706So2d[4]907
706So2d[1]908
710So2d[3]224
e 710So2d225
761So2d430
23FLW(D)481
e 23FLW(D)
[1153
Cir. 7
42F3d[4]1129

—26—
Nechtman v Saker
1972
696So2d964
22FLW(D)
[1815

—31—
Atlas Van Lines Inc. v Rossmoore
1972
635So2d1003

—118—
Belcher Oil Co. v Dade County
1972
677So2d[5]398
1981FlAG9
1995FlAG2

20FSU860

—132—
Wolfe v Florida
1972
666So2d994
j 722So2d827
723So2d189
23FLW(S)542
j 22FLW(D)
[1300

—136—
Edwards v Fort Walton Beach
1972
e 487So2d[1]320
652So2d1273
714So2d1042
j 724So2d1260
748So2d1103
23FLW(D)
[1351
j 24FLW(D)296

—140—
Russell v Florida
1972
617So2d778
666So2d215

—142—
Bader v Curtis Publishing Co.
1972
j 621So2d554
629So2d857

—146—
Sligar v Tucker
1972
649So2d333

—148—
Kilgore v Florida
1972
613So2d1363
613So2d[6]1364
636So2d[6]870
678So2d[6]460
678So2d[7]460
705So2d[6]104
705So2d[7]104
23FLW(D)264

—163—
Kephart v Pickens
1972
642So2d1155
664So2d[4]18

—170—
Fortenberry v Mandell
1972
646So2d[2]267
699So2d[2]703
718So2d[1]821
22FLW(D)
[1123
22FLW(D)
[2446
23FLW(D)979

—207—
Jefferson National Bank at Sunny Isles v Metropolitan Dade County
1972
648So2d163
667So2d[5]260

—217—
Weiner v Moreno
1973
j 613So2d545
f 629So2d[2]200
639So2d[2]1122
645So2d[2]1110
647So2d898
678So2d921
j 701So2d92
f 719So2d[2]328
730So2d377
j 22FLW(D)
[2162
f 23FLW(D)
[1930
24FLW(D)846
Cir. 11
840FS127

—220—
Merkle v Rice Construction Co.
1973
412So2d[1]874

—227—
Fatolitis v Fatolitis
1973
661So2d[4]92

—461—
Thompson v Commercial Union Insurance Company of New York
1972
Cir. 11
10F3d763

—466—
Stewart v Gilliam
1972
e 397So2d[1]350
651So2d[1]675
652So2d364
665So2d[1]1050

—745—
Firestone v Time Inc.
1972
648So2d242
Cir. 11
896FS1192

—754—
Estate of Stewart v Caldwell
1972
691So2d501
22FLW(D)595

—764—
Panning Lumber and Supply Co. v Sexton
1972
613So2d517
627So2d1333

—771—
Leon Realty Inc. v Bradwell
1972
722So2d[2]957
24FLW(D)98

—775—
Gull Construction Co. v Hendrie
1973
d 622So2d[2]8

—780—
Caplinger v Florida
1973
683So2d[4]1096
45A5602n

—783—
Florida v Lampley
1973
630So2d1142

—796—
Baker v Baker
1973
712So2d1196
23FLW(D)
[1508
Cir. 11
150BRW[4]476

—798—
Smiles v Young
1973
654So2d[1]1187
j 687So2d986
698So2d538
699So2d1043
722So2d218
758So2d1136
22FLW(S)440
j 22FLW(D)477
22FLW(D)
[2340
23FLW(D)
[2287

—808—
Bryant v Small
1973
675So2d[2]1387

—818—
Churruca v Miami Jai-Alai Inc.
1973
413So2d[1]55

Vol. 272

—1—
Salas v Liberty Mutual Fire Insurance Co.
1972
640So2d159
682So2d[4]686
708So2d[4]681
708So2d[5]681
753So2d83
j 753So2d89
23FLW(D)948

—9—
Hollander v Nolan Brown Motors Inc.
1973
650So2d[2]77
653So2d[2]481

—14—
Wood v Wood
1973
698So2d[1]813
22FLW(S)329

—19—
Traud v Walk
1973
739So2d713
e 746So2d[1]113

e= explained
f= followed
d= distinguished
volume #
page #
case name of cited case
headnote reference
j= dissenting opinion

figure 12 (continued)

SOUTHERN REPORTER, 2d SERIES (Florida Cases) — **Vol. 272**

—823—
Case 1
Harrison
v Florida
1972

—823—
Case 2
ustin v Austin
1972

—823—
Case 3
DeVoe v
Florida
1972

—823—
Case 4
dom v Florida
1972

—823—
Case 5
outh Broward
Hospital
District v
Williams
1972

—824—
Case 1
Walters v
Florida
1972

—824—
Case 2
Miller v Miller
1972
276So2d169
283So2d559

—824—
Case 3
liami v Radoff
1972

—824—
Case 4
Hawkes v
Hawkes
1972

—825—
Case 1
Mack v Florida
1973

—825—
Case 2
Explosives
Inc. v Atlas
Chemical
Industries Inc.
1973

—825—
Case 3
Sheppard
v Florida
1973

—825—
Case 4
Rector v
Anderson
1973

—826—
Case 1
Garner v
Florida
1973
s 276So2d53

—826—
Case 2
McKenzie v
McKenzie
1973

—826—
Case 3
Florida ex rel
Dames v
Wainwright
1973

—826—
Case 4
Ellis v Ellis
1973

—827—
Case 1
Teaters v
Marion
Petroleum Inc.
1973

—827—
Case 2
Wright v
Florida
1973

—827—
Case 3
Battis v Genung
1973

—827—
Case 4
Fair v Beard
1973

—827—
Case 5
Flores v Florida
1973

—827—
Case 6
Kersey v
Florida
1973

—828—
Case 1
Loray v Florida
1973

—828—
Case 2
McGrath v
New York
1973

—828—
Case 3
O'Leary
v McGuire
1973

—828—
Case 4
Washington
v Florida
1973

—829—
Case 1
Long v Florida
1973

—829—
Case 2
Zenith Life
Insurance
Co. v Jensen
1973

—829—
Case 3
Dialogue
Marketing
Inc. v Tietjen
1973

—829—
Case 4
Pepper v
Florida
1973

—829—
Case 5
Stevenson
v Spears
1973

Vol. 272

—1—
Salas v Liberty
Mutual Fire
Insurance Co.
1972
s 247So2d528
s 273So2d96
276So2d9
288So2d1242
j 288So2d1243
289So2d750
292So2d169
f 316So2d639
319So2d2154
327So2d291
337So2d4831
337So2d5831
340So2d11259
344So2d288
d 344So2d1596
d 344So2d5879
352So2d51173
360So2d21275
363So2d21081
370So2d3398
371So2d2148
373So2d435
390So2d176
390So2d376
j 443So2d432
483So2d5403
512So2d1973
515So2d21324
548So2d2735
567So2d4410
j 567So2d413
d 568So2d1115
12FSU503
30ALR226n
52ALR31n
52ALR98n

—7—
Case 1
Aircraft Taxi
Co. v Ford
1973
28MiL323
55ALR199n

—7—
Case 2
Rushing
v Florida
1973

—8—
Bianchi v
Florida
1973
291So2d122
324So2d1711
332So2d1112
338So2d1250

—9—
Case 1
David v Florida
1973
S 277So2d69

—9—
Case 2
Arline v Grant
1973

—9—
Case 3
Hollander v
Nolan Brown
Motors Inc.
1973
284So2d432
291So2d641
336So2d2459
353So2d1239
31MiL1296

—11—
Case 1
Smith v Florida
1973

—11—
Case 2
Rosselet v I &
H Realty Corp.
1973

[handwritten annotations:] same case. — headnote — f=followed

70

figure 12 (continued)

FLW(S)686	**Vol. 263**	785So2d1212	—853—	—751—	**Vol. 273**

—492—
3So2d593

—509—
3So2d[3]417

—541—
So2d[1]1085

ol. 261

—1—
So2d[3]1169
1FlAG45

-129—
So2d[3]523

-146—
So2d204
So2d1251
So2d890

-172—
So2d1114

801—
5o2d523

832—
1FlaApp
[LX[4]13464
1FlaApp
[LX[5]13464
5o2d[4]191
5o2d[5]191
_W(D)[4]
[2330
_W(D)[5]
[2330

l. 262

193—
FlaApp
[LX[1]12169
.FlaApp
[LX[2]12169
.FlaApp
[LX[3]12169
5o2d[1]688
5o2d[2]688
5o2d[3]688
_W(D)[1]
[2117
_W(D)[2]
[2117
_W(D)[3]
[2117

276—
.FlaApp
[LX16042

470—
5o2d701

661—
1FlAG49
1FlAG63
1WLR249

Vol. 263

—1—
2001FlaApp
[LX8070
774So2d824
783So2d320
26FLW(D)
[1480

—218—
2001FlaApp
[LX[2]9144
777So2d1193
j 777So2d1197
784So2d1089
793So2d[2]1010
26FLW(D)[2]
[1647

—223—
771So2d1140

—573—
768So2d19

—629—
773So2d117

—797—
783So2d244
2001FlAG55
2001FlAG56

Vol. 264

—5—
780So2d29
783So2d1059

—57—
789So2d[4]1150

—838—
Sutton v Stear
2001FlaApp
[LX[2]13877
26FLW(D)[2]
[2366

Vol. 265

—5—
780So2d163

—18—
~ 2001FlaApp
[LX15748
788So2d[3]279
Cir. 11
244F3d882
145FS2d1311

—361—
j 2001FL LX
[2209

—685—
cc 2000USDist
[LX1188
2001FL LX[3]
[1750

785So2d1212
26FLW(S)[3]579

—095—
2001FL LX[5]
[1750
26FLW(S)[5]579

—699—
Aron v Huttoe
d 2001FlaApp
[LX13909
2001FlaApp
[LX13925
d 26FLW(D)
[2392
26FLW(D)
[2395

Vol. 266

—61—
Cir. 11
244F3d878

—178—
771So2d1219
d 771So2d1220

—385—
2001FlaApp
[LX16042

Vol. 267

—54—
778So2d1053

—73—
~ 785So2d1275

—105—
Makris v State
Farm Mut.
Auto. Ins. Co.
2001FlaApp
[LX[2]7476
26FLW(D)[2]
[1373

—325—
2001FlaApp
[LX16035

—337—
2001FlaApp
[LX9841
774So2d64
26FLW(D)
[1774

—360—
2001FlaApp
[LX15636

—853—
Beefy Trail, Inc.
v Beefy King
International,
Inc.
Cir. 2
2001USDist
[LX10801
Cir. 11
256BRW[1]158
256BRW[2]158

Vol. 268

—166—
Cir. 11
141FS2d1357

—363—
28FSU491

—410—
Cir. 11
237F3d[2]1329

—529—
2001FL LX[1]
[1747
2001FL LX
[2269
26FLW(S)[1]573

Vol. 269

—9—
773So2d100

—70—
2001FlaApp
[LX7933
791So2d44
26FLW(D)
[1458

—714—
Cir. 2
2001USDist
[LX10801

—753—
Cir. 3
2000USDist
[LX5719
2000USDist
[LX8697

Vol. 270

—399—
785So2d[1]746

—451—
85A518n

—455—
781So2d522

—751—
Tropicana
Pools, Inc. v
Brown
2001FlaApp
[LX11490
791So2d1217
26FLW(D)
[2020

Vol. 271

—7—
777So2d420

—31—
773So2d[4]589

—118—
2000FlaApp
[LX8472
2001FlaApp
[LX7482
779So2d514
f 781So2d1139
25FLW(D)
[1637
26FLW(D)
[1360
2001FlAG44

—132—
785So2d[4]745

—136—
773So2d[1]589

—148—
773So2d603

—207—
787So2d925

—466—
2001FlaApp
[LX11854
26FLW(D)
[2028

—787—
2001FlaApp
[LX7825
790So2d475
26FLW(D)
[1411

—796—
788So2d1086

Vol. 272

—129—
774So2d933

—486—
Cir. 11
2001USDist
[LX17303

—841—
768So2d[2]517
f 768So2d518

Vol. 273

—70—
2001FlaApp
[LX16038

—83—
Orlando Sports
Stadium, Inc. v
Sentinel Star
Co.
779So2d[1]600

—117—
Cir. 11
2001USDist
[LX14489

Vol. 274

—29—
783So2d299

—256—
f 2000FlaApp
[LX16969
j 2000FlaApp
[LX16969
f 2001FlaApp
[LX4121
2001FlaApp
[LX8274
2001FlaApp
[LX12509
2001FlaApp
[LX14205
768So2d1053
769So2d493
770So2d[3]663
770So2d[4]663
770So2d1285
774So2d933
775So2d[3]931
778So2d450
778So2d[3]451
778So2d1055
778So2d[3]1056
779So2d401
784So2d435
f 784So2d437
784So2d455
787So2d758
793So2d1112
f 26FLW(D)139
j 26FLW(D)139
f 26FLW(D)956
26FLW(D)
[1573
26FLW(D)
[2161
26FLW(D)
[2426

—517—
782So2d432

—522—
769So2d967

note that the cited case was not mentioned in any case for this volume of Shepard's.

103

Figure 13: Shepard's Citations for statutes (key to abbreviations)

ABBREVIATIONS—ANALYSIS
STATUTES

Form of Statute

Amend.	Amendment	¶	Paragraph
Art.	Article	P.L.	Public Law
C or Ch.	Chapter	Proc.	Proclamation
CCJR	Conference Committee Joint Resolution	Res.	Resolution
		§	Section
Cl.	Clause	S. B.	Senate Bill
Ex.	Extra Session	S. C. R.	Senate Concurrent Resolution
Ex. Ord.	Executive Order		
H. B.	House Bill	S. J. R.	Senate Joint Resolution
H. C. R.	House Concurrent Resolution	S. M.	Senate Memorial
		Sp	Special Acts or Laws
H. J. R.	House Joint Resolution	S. R.	Senate Resolution
H. M.	House Memorial	St.	Statutes at Large
H. R.	House Resolution	Stat.	Florida Statutes
J. R.	Joint Resolution	Subd.	Subdivision
No.	Number	Sub ¶	Subparagraph
p	Page	Subsec.	Subsection

Operation of Statute

Legislative

A	(amended)	Statute amended.
Ad	(added)	New section added.
E	(extended)	Provisions of an existing statute extended in their application to a later statute, or allowance of additional time for performance of duties required by a statute within a limited time.
L	(limited)	Provisions of an existing statute declared not to be extended in their application to a later statute.
R	(repealed)	Abrogation of an existing statute.
Re-en	(re-enacted)	Statute re-enacted.
Rn	(renumbered)	Renumbering of existing sections.
Rp	(repealed in part)	Abrogation of part of an existing statute.
Rs	(repealed and superseded)	Abrogation of an existing statute and substitution of new legislation therefor.
Rv	(revised)	Statute revised.
S	(superseded)	Substitution of new legislation for an existing statute not expressly abrogated.
Sd	(suspended)	Statute suspended.
Sdp	(suspended in part)	Statute suspended in part.
Sg	(supplementing)	New matter added to an existing statute.
Sp	(superseded in part)	Substitution of new legislation for part of an existing statute expressly abrogated.
Va	(validated)	

Judicial

C	Constitutional.		V	Void or invalid.
U	Unconstitutional.		Va	Valid.
Up	Unconstitutional in part.		Vp	Void or invalid in part.

ABBREVIATIONS—COURTS

Cir. DC–U.S. Court of Appeals, District of Columbia Circuit
Cir. (number)–U.S. Court of Appeals Circuit (number)
Cir. Fed.–U.S. Court of Appeals, Federal Circuit
CCPA–Court of Customs and Patents Appeals
CIT–United States Court of International Trade
ClCt–Claims Court (U.S.)
CtCl–Court of Claims (U.S.)
CuCt–Customs Court
ECA–Temporary Emergency Court of Appeals
ML–Judicial Panel on Multidistrict Litigation
RRR–Special Court Regional Rail Reorganization Act of 1973

§ 34-17 CODE OF VIRGINIA, 1950

87BRW416	15BRW540	7VCO56	**Subsec. 5**	62Geo814
93BRW448	47BRW366	50SE272	7VCO56	
103BRW736	14RIC651	416SE232	Cir. 4	**Subsec. b**
105BRW11	37W&L139	Cir. 4	560FS793	221Va1040
123BRW742	39W&L404	656F2d62	39BRW945	28VCO72
127BRW355	21W&M653	729F2d978	52BRW595	277SE183
129BRW84	63CaL1469	498FS157	71BRW595	68VaL512
145BRW224	62Geo849	2BRW136	25RIC613	
165BRW178		2BRW380	62Geo827	**Subsec. c**

§ 34-23

§ 34-28.1

87BRW416 ... (figure of Shepard's Citations page)

§ 34-17

87BRW416
93BRW448
103BRW736
105BRW11
123BRW742
127BRW355
129BRW84
145BRW224
165BRW178
22RIC530
23RIC573
24RIC758
25RIC609
26RIC647
27RIC629
53VaL1571
68VaL521
37W&L139
21W&M650

Subsec. 1
Cir. 4
715F2d861
96BRW62

§ 34-18
A 1975C466
A 1977C496
A 1990C942
Cir. 4
656F2d62
24RIC758
62Geo800

§ 34-19
A 1975C466
A 1977C496
A 1990C942
24RIC758

§ 34-20
37W&L139

§ 34-21
A 1975C466
A 1977C496
A 1990C942
Cir. 4
260FS449
31BRW757
48BRW314
105BRW11
129BRW84
24RIC758
37W&L139

§ 34-22
194Va318
8VCO407
33VCO186
73SE375
Cir. 3
438FS840
Cir. 4
780F2d411

15BRW540
47BRW366
14RIC651
37W&L139
39W&L404
21W&M653
63CaL1469
62Geo849

§ 34-23
A 1974C272
A 1981C580
194Va318
73SE375
14RIC651
68VaL521
37W&L140

§ 34-24
A 1972C825
A 1974C272
A 1981C580
194Va318
73SE375
Cir. 4
15BRW619
16BRW686
47BRW122
14RIC649
68VaL521
37W&L139
62Geo843

§ 34-25
Cir. 4
10BRW950
37W&L143

§ 34-26 et seq.
Cir. 4
560FS792
46VaL184

§§ 34-26 to 34-28
24RIC758

§ 34-26
A 1956C367
1962C570
1964C28
1966C499
A 1970C428
A 1975C466
A 1976C150
A 1977C253
A 1977C496
A 1990C942
A 1992C644
A 1993C150
188Va573
243Va501

7VCO56
50SE272
416SE232
Cir. 4
656F2d62
729F2d978
498FS157
2BRW136
2BRW380
3BRW244
3BRW641
4BRW121
6BRW263
9BRW992
11BRW693
11BRW775
12BRW51
23BRW124
24BRW147
31BRW758
36BRW313
39BRW366
39BRW945
41BRW947
47BRW367
52BRW207
63BRW256
93BRW447
127BRW373
132BRW313
156BRW24
158BRW56
162BRW735
165BRW178
13RIC225
14RIC640
21RIC531
23RIC571
24RIC758
25RIC613
27RIC629
17W&L24
37W&L129
39W&L404
77MnL617

Subsec. 1
62Geo827

Subsec. 1a
7VCO56
Cir. 4
560FS792
6BRW264

Subsec. 2
Cir. 4
165BRW181

Subsec. 4
Cir. 4
560FS793
6BRW264
162BRW737

Subsec. 4a
Cir. 4
162BRW737

Subsec. 5
7VCO56
Cir. 4
560FS793
39BRW945
52BRW595
71BRW595
25RIC613
62Geo827

Subsec. 6
Cir. 4
127BRW373

Subsec. 7
243Va501
Cir. 4
127BRW373
132BRW313
169BRW582

Subsec. 8
Cir. 4
156BRW23
Subd. a
Cir. 4
156BRW24

§ 34-27
A 1956C637
1962C570
1964C28
1966C499
A 1970C428
A 1977C496
A 1993C150
188Va573
50SE272
Cir. 4
656F2d62
498FS157
560FS793
2BRW136
36BRW314
60BRW170
75BRW358
93BRW447
158BRW56
169BRW582
14RIC644
21RIC531
22RIC532
23RIC571
17W&L24
37W&L129

§ 34-28
A 1992C644
Cir. 4
560FS792
132BRW313
156BRW24
22RIC320
37W&L147
39W&L404

§ 34-28.1
Ad 1990C942
A 1991C256
A 1993C150
A 1994C35
Cir. 4
151BRW79
158BRW56
158BRW963
158BRW964
24RIC758
25RIC615
27RIC629

§ 34-29
1952C377
A 1952C432
A 1954C143
A 1954C379
A 1958C217
A 1958C417
A 1960C498
1966C499
A 1970C428
A 1978C564
A 1992C674
188Va573
221Va1040
3VaA86
28VCO70
50SE272
277SE183
277SE184
348SE407
Cir. 3
634F2d92
Cir. 4
675F2d615
559FS316
574FS968
7BRW893
15BRW539
47BRW366
159BRW759
162BRW735
22RIC567
46VaL1661
56VaL1393
17W&L24
28W&L94
37W&L129
37W&L142
53CaL252

Subsec. a
221Va1040
223Va521
28VCO72
277SE183
290SE864
Cir. 4
162BRW742
Cir. 6
423FS33
68VaL512
37W&L134

62Geo814

Subsec. b
221Va1040
28VCO72
277SE183
68VaL512

Subsec. c
221Va1040
277SE184
37W&L137

Subsec. d
34VCO193
Cir. 4
559FS323
162BRW742

Subsec. e
56VaL1394
37W&L134
62Geo849

Subsec. f
219Va609
34VCO192
249SE180
Cir. 4
164BRW260
17RIC763
37W&L134

§ 34-30
A 1952C257
A 1954C143
A 1956C621
Rs 1970C428

§ 34-31
A 1974C272
Cir. 4
8BRW151
83BRW409

§ 34-32
A 1954C613
A 1974C272
37W&L148
62Geo839

§ 34-34
Ad 1990C425
A 1992C716
23VCO345
Cir. 4
162BRW735
165BRW178
24RIC758
25RIC609
26RIC822
28RIC1007
94WVL455

Subsec. A
25RIC609

1028

Annotations:
- Statute section number
- Amended in 1993, Chapter 150
- Supreme Court case found at Volume 243, Page 501 Virginia Reports
- Repealed and Superceded
- Law Review Reference
- Added in 1990, Chapter 425

AMERICAN LAW REPORTS 6

American Law Reports, or *A.L.R.* as they are more commonly known, are sets of books published by Lawyers Co-operative Publishing Company that report on specific legal topics. These reports are known as *annotations* but should not to be confused with annotations in statutes and codes. Unlike those in statutes and codes, *A.L.R.* annotations are not just abstracts, or summaries, about cases.

Instead, *A.L.R.* annotations are comprehensive studies on the topics chosen. Each report is preceded by a case opinion, which the editors believe would be of importance to lawyers and other legal professionals. The annotation follows the printed case and expounds on the issue presented by the court in the printed case.

The annotations track the development of the issue from its beginnings in our legal system to the date of publication. It does this by citing and analyzing other cases from all jurisdictions that discuss or relate to the issue in the printed case. These annotations are sweeping reports on important issues and can be a wealth of information if they pertain to your problem. (see Figure 15 on pages 80 to 81.)

How to Find American Law Reports

American Law Reports are printed in six sets: *American Law Reports*, (abbreviated A.L.R.), *American law Reports, Second Series* (abbreviated A.L.R.2d, and sometimes referred to as "Second Series"), *American Law Reports,Third Series* (A.L.R.3d, or "Third Series"), *American Law Reports, Fourth Series* (A.L.R.4th, or "Fourth Series"), *American Law Reports, Fifth Series* (A.L.R.5th, or "Fifth Series") and *American Law Reports, Federal* (A.L.R. Fed.). (To avoid confusion, a reference to "*A.L.R.*," (in italics) relates to all sets of *American Law Reports*, regardless of which series; and a reference to "A.L.R.," or "A.L.R. (first series)," relates only to the first set of books (not to the *Second Series, Third Series, etc.*).)

So, how would you find an annotation pertaining to your particular problem? You certainly would not want to start with volume one of A.L.R. (first series), and work your way through each set. A digest will not help you and neither will the topic and key number system. There are multiple research methods that will lead you to an annotation.

THE INDEX
METHOD

A.L.R. comes complete with a multiple volume index that covers all the sets with the exception of A.L.R. (first series), which is indexed separately. These indexes are updated by pocket parts printed annually. (see Figure 16 on page 84.)

Searching by the index method requires you to follow the information on how to search in an index in Chapter 1. As you can see in Figure 16, the index lists all annotations pertaining to the topic—in this case alimony. If you were interested in the annotation circled, you would go to Volume 98 of A.L.R.3d at page 453.

NOTE: *Page 453 refers to the first page of the annotation, not the case. You must go back to page 445 to read the case that is the basis for the annotation.*

THE DIGEST
METHOD

A.L.R. also comes with a set of digests. A.L.R. (first series) and Second Series have their own digests while the Third, Fourth, and Fifth Series

and A.L.R. Federal are combined. (See Figure 17 on page 85.) As you can see, the digests are separated into topics. In this case, when you look up alimony, you are referred to "divorce and separation." Each topic begins with an index to the annotations and lists abstracts of cases printed in the volumes as well as any annotations that pertain directly to that topic.

SHEPARD'S
CITATOR
METHOD

Shepard's lists any A.L.R. annotation that cites the case you are shepardizing. For example, the cases outlined in Figure 18 (on page 86), make reference to multiple *A.L.R.* citations. Additionally, *Shepard's* has a citator dedicated solely to *American Law Reports*. You may want to use them if you believe you have exhausted your other avenues of case method searching. (See Chapter 5 for specific instructions on how to shepardize.) Be aware that *Shepard's* for *American Law Reports* is not printed in the usual color scheme for *Shepard's*. All volumes are in the same greenish-olive color of *American Law Reports* instead.

UPDATING AMERICAN LAW REPORTS

American Law Reports has gone through many mutations regarding its method of updating. Do not let this confuse you. It may help to think of each series as a separate set of books.

BLUE BOOK OF
SUPPLEMENTAL
DECISIONS

These volumes supplement A.L.R. (first series). When you locate an annotation in A.L.R. (first series), you then go to the A.L.R. *Blue Book* and look up that citation again. It will cite all other cases that have been written since the original annotation. For example, look at Figure 19 on page 87. Once you obtain these citations, you can look them up and determine if the law has changed since the annotation in A.L.R. (first series) was written. The *Blue Book of Supplemental Decisions* is updated by an annual pamphlet.

A.L.R. 2D
LATER CASE
SERVICE

American Law Reports, Second Series, does not use the *Blue Book of Supplemental Decisions*. Instead, it is updated by the *Later Case Service*. Unlike the *Blue Book of Supplemental Decisions*, it not only lists any case

citations that arose since the publication of an annotation, it also digests the cases and indexes them to the exact section of the A.L.R.2d annotation they are meant to update. This enables you to see directly where the law has been expanded or changed. (See Figure 20 on page 88.)

POCKET PARTS

Cases that update the annotations in A.L.R.3d, A.L.R.4th, A.L.R. 5th and A.L.R. Fed. may be found in annual pocket part supplements. You will not need to consult a separate set of books like for A.L.R. (first series) and Second Series. You use the pocket part in the same manner as you do for digests.

One important point to remember about A.L.R.5th and A.L.R. Fed. is that new volumes are still being published. You will need to consult any new volumes printed after the date of the pocket part to determine if there is updated information on any topic that is not reflected in the pocket part.

SUPERSEDING ANNOTATIONS

Assume that you found an annotation in A.L.R.2d. Later cases (found in the *Later Case Service*) indicate that the issue discussed in the annotation has been completely changed by the newer case opinions. So, the annotation in A.L.R.2d, while giving you a foundation for your problem and historical background of the law, is not going to be of any additional help.

It would be helpful to find out if the *American Law Reports* editors wrote a new annotation—one that discusses the law in the past (superceded) *and* currently (supplemented). There are two ways to see if the annotation was either *superseded* or *supplemented*.

One is to look up the annotation as you would to update for newer cases. The *Blue Book for Supplemental Decisions*, A.L.R.2d *Later Case Service*, and pocket parts for A.L.R.3d, A.L.R.4th and A.L.R. Fed. all refer to the latest annotations available on the same topic. In addition, you may refer to the *Annotation History Table*. This table is found in the last volume of the "Index to Annotations." (see Figure 21 on page 89.) If the table says "supplemented" you will read both annotations, while if it says "superseded," you would only have to read the newer

annotation. Most annotations in A.L.R.3d, A.L.R.4th and A.L.R. Fed. will be superseded instead of merely supplemented. Most supplemented materials refer to A.L.R. (first series) and Second Series.

For example, as shown in Figure 21, 90 A.L.R.4th 586, was superseded by 72 A.L.R.5th 403. You only need to read 72 A.L.R.5th 403 to get the full import of the topic being discussed in the annotation. If, however, it had said "supplemented" you would have had to read both 90 A.L.R.4th 586 and 72 A.L.R.5th 403.

American Law Reports can be a very helpful resource for you. It is most helpful when you know what your problem really is about. Then A.L.R. may give you an abundance of information, covering an issue like yours in minute detail. It is also beneficial, however, when you have only a vague idea about what your problem entails. Then the annotations may help you frame your issue more clearly. After reading an annotation, you may get more ideas, learn more words and phrases concerning your problem, and want to go back to doing case research in the digests. Sometimes all your research will need to get on the right course is someone else's point of view on a subject. *American Law Reports* annotations provide that point of view.

ANNOTATION

DIVORCED WOMAN'S SUBSEQUENT SEXUAL RELATIONS OR MISCONDUCT AS WARRANTING, ALONE OR WITH OTHER CIRCUMSTANCES, MODIFICATION OF ALIMONY DECREE

I. PRELIMINARY MATTERS

§ 1. Introduction:
    [a] Scope
    [b] Related matters
§ 2. Summary and comment:
    [a] Generally
    [b] Practice pointers

II. SPECIFIC SEXUAL RELATIONS

A. LIVING WITH LOVER

1. MODIFICATION UNDER STATUTORY PROVISIONS

§ 3. Statute providing for modification for cohabitation—without more

---

TOTAL CLIENT-SERVICE LIBRARY® REFERENCES

24 Am Jur 2d, Divorce and Separation §§ 685–88

8 Am Jur Pl & Pr Forms (rev), Divorce and Separation, Forms 611-16

1 Am Jur Legal Forms 2d, Alimony and Separation Agreements §§ 17:21–17:26, 17:71–17:83

1 Am Jur Proof of Facts 237, Adultery; 1 Am Jur Proof of Facts 421, Alimony, Proof 4; 17 Am Jur Proof of Facts 2d 345, Forensic Economics—Use of Economists in Cases of Dissolution of Marriage

17 Am Jur Trials 721, Defense Against Wife's Action for Support

US L Ed Digest, Divorce and Separation § 8

ALR Digests, Divorce and Separation §§ 95–105

L Ed Index to Annos, Divorce and Separation

ALR Quick Index, Alimony; Divorce and Separation; Sexual Relations and Offenses; Subsequent Acts or Events

Federal Quick Index, Alimony; Divorce and Separation; Sexual Relations and Offenses

---

Consult POCKET PART in this volume for later cases

453

ALIMONY—DIVORCED WIFE'S SEXUAL MISCONDUCT   98 ALR3d
98 ALR3d 453

§ 4. —With additional requirement that ex-wife hold herself out as her
        lover's wife:
        [a] Conduct sufficient to authorize or affect modification
        [b] Conduct insufficient to authorize or affect modification
        [c] —Effect of terms of incorporated separation agreement
        [d] —Lesbian relationship

2. MODIFICATION WHERE NO STATUTORY PROVISIONS APPLICABLE

§ 5. Without change in financial circumstances:
        [a] Conduct sufficient to authorize or affect modification
        [b] Conduct insufficient to authorize or affect modification
§ 6. With changed financial circumstances—wife receiving support from lover
§ 7. —Wife supporting lover
§ 8. —Other changes in financial circumstances

B. SEXUAL RELATIONS WITHOUT COHABITATION

§ 9. Generally:
        [a] Conduct sufficient to authorize or affect modification
        [b] Conduct insufficient to authorize or affect modification
§ 10. In combination with changed financial circumstances
§ 11. Prostitution

III. NON-SEXUAL, UNSPECIFIED, OR GENERALIZED CHARGES OF MISCON-
        DUCT

§ 12. Violation of court order:
        [a] Conduct sufficient to authorize or affect modification
        [b] Conduct insufficient to authorize or affect modification
§ 13. Interference with former husband's economic interests
§ 14. Hostile actions toward former husband's present wife
§ 15. Alcoholism or excessive drinking
§ 16. Squandering alimony:
        [a] Conduct sufficient to authorize or affect modification
        [b] Conduct insufficient to authorize or affect modification
§ 17. Other or unspecified misconduct:
        [a] Conduct sufficient to warrant or affect modification
        [b] Conduct insufficient to warrant or affect modification

---

INDEX

Accommodations, effect of sharing of
    upon obligation to pay spousal support,
    §§ 4[a], 5[a, b]
Alcoholism or excessive drinking, effect
    of, §§ 5[a], 15, 16
Apartment, applying for as man and wife,
    § 4[a]
"Assertive conduct" as married couple,
    § 4[b]

Bastards, effect of birth of, § 8
Bad check, effect of former wife being
    arrested for passing, § 17[a]
Board and rent, effect of payment of to
    cohabitor upon modification proceed-
    ings, §§ 3, 5[b]
Care and maintenance, necessity that co-
    habitor assume responsibility for,
    §§ 4[a,b], 5[b]

Figure 15:(continued)

Since relevant statutes are included only to the extent that they are reflected in the reported cases within the scope of this annotation, the reader is advised to consult the latest enactments of pertinent jurisdictions.

[b] Related matters

Adulterous wife's right to permanent alimony. 86 ALR3d 97.

Fault as consideration in alimony, spousal support, or property division awards pursuant to no-fault divorce. 86 ALR3d 1116.

Divorce: Power of court to modify decree to alimony or support of spouse which was based on agreement of parties. 61 ALR3d 520.

Retrospective increase in allowance for alimony, separate maintenance, or support. 52 ALR3d 156.

Effect of remarriage of spouses to each other on permanent alimony provisions in final divorce decree. 52 ALR3d 1334.

Alimony as affected by wife's remarriage, in absence of controlling specific statute. 48 ALR2d 270.

Remarriage of wife as affecting husband's obligation under separation agreement to support her or make other money payments to her. 48 ALR2d 318.

Reconciliation as affecting decree for alimony. 35 ALR2d 741.

Change in financial condition or needs of husband or wife as ground for modification of decree for alimony or maintenance. 18 ALR2d 10.

Misconduct of wife to whom divorce is decreed as affecting allowance of alimony, or amount allowed. 9 ALR2d 1026.

Husband's default, contempt, or other misconduct as affecting modification of decree for alimony, separate maintenance, or support. 6 ALR2d 835.

Retrospective modification of or refusal to enforce decree for alimony, separate maintenance, or support. 6 ALR2d 1277.

Wife's misconduct or fault as affecting her right to temporary alimony or suit money. 2 ALR2d 307.

§ 2. Summary and comment

[a] Generally

Generally, where statutes allow modification, both judicially determined alimony awards and those based on contractual provisions incorporated in a decree are modifiable by the court where there has been a substantial change in the circumstances of at least one of the parties.[7] Usually the change in circumstances required is a financial one, but the divorced wife's subsequent sexual relations or misconduct may warrant, in itself, or in combination with other circumstances, the modification of an alimony decree, as shown by the cases discussed in this annotation.

The courts have frequently decided or discussed the question whether a finding of extramarital sexual relations on the part of a divorced wife warranted or was relevant to a modification of a decree for alimony, both under and in the absence of applicable statutory provisions.[8] Where the former wife was living with another, one of two general types of statutory provisions were involved. Under one type of statute allowing modification for cohabitation without any further requirements, the former wife's con-

---

ments are often brought as suits to modify private contract obligations, and are thus not within the scope of this annotation.

458

7. See generally, 24 Am Jur 2d, Divorce and Separation §§ 675 et seq.

8. §§ 3–11, infra.

duct in living with a paramour has been held sufficient to warrant, or to be relevant to, modification of the decree.[9] Under the second type of statute, which allowed modification for cohabitation of an ex-wife with a lover and also required that she hold herself out as her lover's wife, it has been held that the former wife's conduct was sufficient to warrant, or was relevant to, modification;[10] and her conduct has also been held to be insufficient, under the circumstances involved, to authorize or affect such modification.[11] Specific circumstances resulting in such a holding include a separation agreement which was stipulated to be nonmodifiable,[12] but not when the former wife's lover was a lesbian, since then the relationship did not fall within the statutory requirement that the woman live with a man and hold herself out as his wife.[13]

Where no specific statutory provisions were applicable and where no changes in financial circumstances were shown, the former wife's conduct in living with a lover was held sufficient to warrant, or to be relevant to, modification of a decree for alimony,[14] although it has also frequently been held to be insufficient.[15]

Where changed financial circumstances were also present, courts have held that the former wife's conduct in living with a lover warranted, or was relevant to, modification of the de-cree, not only where the changed financial circumstances involved their relationship, as where the former wife was receiving support from her lover[16] or was supporting him,[17] but also where the change in financial circumstances did not involve their relationship.[18]

Where the former wife has indulged in sexual relations without cohabitation, this has been held both sufficient[19] and insufficient[20] to warrant, or to be relevant to, modification of a decree for alimony. But where the sexual relations have occurred in combination with changed financial circumstances,[21] or and where the sexual relations indulged in amounted to prostitution,[22] the courts have likewise held that this was sufficient to warrant or be relevant to modification of such a decree.

The courts have also frequently dealt with charges of nonsexual misconduct. One of the charges most frequently involved is the claim that the former wife violated a visitation or custody order; the courts have held such conduct sufficient, if proved, to warrant, or to be relevant to, modification of an order for alimony.[23] although others have held the contrary.[24]

The ex-wife's interference with the former husband's economic interests[25] or her hostile action towards his pres-

---

9. § 3, infra.

10. § 4[a], infra.

11. § 4[b–d], infra.

12. § 4[c], infra.

13. § 4[d], infra.

14. § 5[a], infra.

15. § 5[b], infra.

16. § 6, infra.

17. § 7, infra.

18. § 8, infra.

19. § 9[a], infra.

20. § 9[b], infra.

21. § 10, infra.

22. § 11, infra.

23. § 12[a], infra.

24. § 12[b], infra.

25. § 13, infra.

Figure 16: A.L.R. Index

ALIMONY—Cont'd
Bankruptcy—Cont'd
other allowances in divorce or
separation suit as passing, or exempt
from passing, to trustee in wife's
bankruptcy, under § 70(a) of Bankruptcy Act (11 U.S.C.A. § 110(a)),
10 ALR Fed 881
Bigamy, permanent alimony, right to
allowance in connection with decree of
annulment, **81 ALR3d 281**
Cohabitation
divorced wife's subsequent sexual relations or misconduct as warranting,
alone or with other circumstances,
modification of alimony decree, **98
ALR3d 453**
palimony, order awarding temporary
support or living expenses upon
separation of unmarried partners
pending contract action based on
services relating to personal relationship, **35 ALR4th 409**
separation agreement, divorced or
separated spouse's living with
member of opposite sex as affecting
other spouse's obligation of alimony
or support under separation agreement, **47 ALR4th 38**
Combined award
allocation or apportionment of previous
combined award of alimony and
child support, **78 ALR2d 1110**
excessiveness or adequacy of amount
awarded for alimony and child support combined, **27 ALR4th 1038**
Contempt proceedings
foreign decree, decree for alimony
rendered in another state or country
(or domestic decree based thereon)
as subject to enforcement by equitable remedies or by contempt
proceedings, **18 ALR2d 862**
jurisdiction, right to punish for
contempt for failure to obey alimony
decree either beyond power or jurisdiction of court or merely erroneous,
12 ALR2d 1059
parties, who may institute civil
contempt proceeding arising out of
matrimonial action, **61 ALR2d 1095**

ALIMONY—Cont'd
Contempt proceedings—Cont'd
pleading and burden of proof, in
contempt proceedings, as to ability
to comply with order for payment of
alimony or child support, **53 ALR2d
591**
Counterclaim and setoff, spouse's right to
set off debt owed by other spouse
against accrued spousal or child support
payments, **11 ALR5th 259**
Death
husband's death as affecting alimony,
39 ALR2d 1406
obligor spouse's death as affecting
alimony, **79 ALR4th 10**
Delinquent or overdue payments
debt, right of spouse to set off debt
owed by other spouse against
accrued spousal or child support
payments, **11 ALR5th 259**
interest on unpaid alimony, **33 ALR2d
1455**
laches or acquiescence as defense, so
as to bar recovery of arrearages of
permanent alimony or child support,
5 ALR4th 1015
visitation, withholding visitation rights
for failure to make alimony or support payments, **65 ALR4th 1155**
Dentists and dentistry
extraordinary expenses, **39 ALR4th
502**
license or professional degree of
spouse as marital property for
purposes of alimony, support or
property settlement, **4 ALR4th 1294**
Depreciation, treatment of depreciation
expenses claimed for tax or accounting
purposes in determining ability to pay
child or spousal support, **28 ALR5th 46,
§ 14–16**
Desertion, see group Abandonment of
person in this topic
Discrimination, statute expressly allowing
alimony to wife, but not expressly
allowing alimony to husband, as unconstitutional sex discrimination, **85
ALR3d 940**

Consult POCKET PART for Later Annotations

DIVORCE AND SEPARATION

§ 65

Consult pocket part for later cases

Laches or acquiescence as defense, so as to bar recovery or arrearages of permanent alimony or child support, 5 ALR4th 1015

Spouse's professional decree or license as marital property for purposes of alimony, support, or property settlement, 4 ALR4th 1294

Divorced woman's subsequent sexual relations or misconduct as warranting, alone or with other circumstances, modification of alimony decree, 98 ALR3d 453

Propriety in divorce proceedings of awarding rehabilitative alimony, 97 ALR3d 740

Fault as consideration in alimony, spousal support, or property division awards pursuant to no-fault divorce, 86 ALR3d 1116

Adulterous wife's right to permanent alimony, 86 ALR3d 97

Statute expressly allowing alimony to wife, but not expressly allowing alimony to husband, as unconstitutional sex discrimination, 85 ALR3d 940

Right to allowance of permanent alimony in connection with decree of annulment, 81 ALR3d 281

Divorce: power of court to modify decree for alimony or support of spouse which was based on agreement of parties, 61 ALR3d 520

Wife's possession of independent means as affecting her right to alimony pendente lite, 60 ALR3d 728

Divorce: provision in decree that one party obtain or maintain life insurance for benefit of other party or child, 59 ALR3d 9

Effect of remarriage of spouses to each other on permanent alimony provisions in final divorce decree, 52 ALR3d 1334

Retrospective increase in allowance for alimony, separate maintenance, or support, 52 ALR3d 156

Divorce or separation: consideration of tax liability or consequences in determining alimony or property settlement provisions, 51 ALR3d 461

Valid foreign divorce as affecting local order previously entered for separate maintenance, 49 ALR3d 1266

Annulment of later marriage as reviving prior husband's obligations under alimony decree or separation agreement, 45 ALR3d 1033

Right of child to enforce provisions for his benefit in parents' separation or property settlement agreement, 34 ALR3d 1357

Spouse's acceptance of payments under alimony or property settlement or child support provisions of divorce judgment as precluding appeal therefrom, 29 ALR3d 1184

Court's establishment of trust to secure alimony or child support in divorce proceedings, 3 ALR3d 1170

Propriety and effect of undivided award for support of more than one person, 2 ALR3d 596

Adequacy or excessiveness of amount of money granted as combined award of alimony and child support, 2 ALR3d 537

Adequacy of amount of money awarded as child support (cases since 1946), 1 ALR3d 324

Adequacy or excessiveness of amount of money awarded as temporary alimony (cases since 1946), 1 ALR3d 280

Adequacy or excessiveness of amount of money awarded as separate maintenance, alimony, or support for wife where no absolute divorce is or has been granted, 1 ALR3d 208

Adequacy of amount of money awarded as permanent alimony where divorce is or has been granted (cases since 1946), 1 ALR3d 123

Excessiveness of amount of money awarded as permanent alimony where divorce is or has been granted (cases since 1946), 1 ALR3d 6

Construction and application of 42 USCS § 659(a) authorizing garnishment against United States or District of Columbia for enforcement of child support and alimony obligations, 44 ALR Fed 494

Auto-Cite®: Cases and annotations referred to herein can be further researched through the Auto-Cite® computer-assisted research service. Use Auto-Cite to check citations for form, parallel references, prior and later history, and annotation references.

———

A statute relating to an allowance from a husband's property to the wife in her action for divorce from bed and board does not create a charge upon the husband's estate or property. *Accardi v Accardi (1964) 97 RI 336, 197 A2d 755, 10 ALR3d 206.*

Payments for separate maintenance become vested when they become due and cannot be modified thereafter. *Porter v Porter (1966) 101 Ariz 131, 416 P2d 564, 34 ALR3d 933, cert den 386 US 957, 18 L Ed 2d 107, 87 S Ct 1028, reh den 386 US 1027, 18 L Ed 2d 472, 87 S Ct 1371.*

That a husband entered into an improvident agreement relating to the amount of alimony is not grounds for relief from a divorce decree incorporating such agreement. *Armstrong v Armstrong (1970) 248 Ark 835, 454 SW2d 660, 61 ALR3d 511.*

[Annotated]

A state statute, which provided that if the wife has not been at fault and has not sufficient means for her support the court may allow her alimony out of the property and earnings of the husband, did not unconstitutionally discriminate against husbands by placing an obligation upon male spouses but no express like obligation upon female spouses. In the absence of a positive legislative statement to the effect that divorced husbands could not claim alimony and in the absence of a case where the husband had been denied or had ever applied for alimony after a divorce, and in view of the fact that alimony for the divorced husband was once available by virtue of a positive state statute,

57

Figure 18: Shepard's Citations (with A.L.R. references)

Vol. 537   SOUTHERN REPORTER, 2d SERIES (Florida Cases)

—125—

Henderson v
Henderson
1988

s 542So2d989

—129—

Cigna v United
Storage
Systems Inc.
1988

cc 549So2d252

—130—

Schmitz v
S.A.B.T.C.
Townhouse
Association Inc.
1988

540So2d912
559So2d¹1161
604So2d1285

—132—

Parham v
Reddick
1988

548So2d⁵696

—137—

Lumbermens
Mutual
Casualty Co. v
Florczyk
1988

s 545So2d1367
FCLM§ 19.05

—138—

Keith v Keith
1988

59A39s
79A22n
79A25n
79A69n

—140—

Xerographics
Inc. v Thomas
1988

545So2d¹928
e 550So2d564
550So2d⁶565
f 551So2d¹506
e 551So2d²506

---

f 551So2d²506
e 551So2d³506
f 551So2d³506
e 551So2d⁴506
f 551So2d⁴506
j 551So2d511
f 557So2d¹940
f 557So2d²940
557So2d⁴941
573So2d1028
579So2d133
j 579So2d135
610So2d19
Cir. 5
788FS¹290
788FS²293
Cir. 11
f 874F2d⁶1583
138BRW¹626
19FSU1115
19FSU1135
41A15s
43A94s
61A397s

—144—

Ferguson
v Florida
1989

541So2d¹1261
550So2d1177
571So2d¹101

—145—

Zubi
Advertising
Services Inc. v
Florida
Department
of Labor and
Unemployment
Security
1989

559So2d¹667

—148—

E.B. v Florida
1989

536So2d⁴372
33A798s

—150—

Tarrant v
Florida
1989

s 544So2d201
40FlS2d124

—153—

Florida v Jones
1989

r 559So2d1096

—154—

1155
Investment
Co. v Tamarac
Club Inc.
1989

—155—

Lichtman v
Lichtman
1989

—156—

Polk v
Crittenden
1989

565So2d⁸1342
571So2d55

—160—

Olenek v
Bennett
1989

—162—

Fowler v
Unemployment
Appeals
Commission
1989

s 545So2d1367
d 571So2d¹1311
1991FlAG98

—164—

Ehrlich v
Ehrlich
1989

—165—

Case 1

Knight v
Florida
1989

—165—

Case 2

Berg v Newton
1989

—168—

School Board
of Pinellas
County v Smith
1989

—170—

Amazon
v Florida
1989

s 547So2d1209
cc 436So2d195
cc 487So2d8
cc 479US914
cc 93LE288
cc 107SC314
559So2d375
578So2d840
Cir. 11
979F2d812

—171—

Case 1

Gray v
Crawford
1989

s 542So2d1733

—171—

Case 2

Florida v Hall
1989

557So2d894
586So2d380

—173—

In the Interest
of T.D.
1989

s 501So2d93
547So2d²984
561So2d359
e 561So2d³360
577So2d572
f 580So2d³895
j 580So2d896
1A565n

—176—

Wilson v
Florida
1989

—177—

Reid v Wilson
Bottling Corp.
1989

—178—

Florida v Sipe
1989

603So2d¹65
603So2d²65
603So2d³65

—180—

Brown v
Florida
1989

545So2d446
558So2d¹545
562So2d³696
587So2d⁴661
598So2d⁴275
607So2d⁴487
13A1240s

—182—

Mrha v Circuit
Court for
Broward
County
1989

50FlS2d62

—185—

McDonald
v Florida
1989

576So2d⁴392

—187—

Harris v
Florida
1989

576So2d899

—188—

Devoe v
Western Auto
Supply Co.
1989

576So2d417
59A1379s

—190—

Schwartz
v Hughes
Supply Inc.
1989

583So2d779
30COA449§ 7

—192—

Florida v Davis
1989

cc 538So2d537
544So2d³245
554So2d²653
557So2d¹161
579So2d¹276
581So2d920

—193—

Case 1

Thomas v
Florida
1989

—193—

Case 2

Baker v Florida
1989

—194—

Hamilton
v Florida
1989

549So2d1129
564So2d²165

—195—

Williams
v Florida
1989

559So2d¹609
575So2d754

ALR references

Aldrich v N. Y. 208 Misc 930. 145 NYS2d 732.
Kingsville Independent School Dist. v. C. (Tex Civ App) 252 SW2d 1022.

83 ALR 1446–1498

Torosian v P. (Ariz) 313 P2d 382 (citing anno).
Krinsky v M. (NH) 128 A2d 915.
Mayo v. M. (Tex Civ App) 269 SW2d 434.

84 ALR 43–100

Supplemented 26 ALR2d 1227.✦

84 ALR 114–117

Hawley v P. C. B. Inc. 345 Mich 500, 76 NW2d 835.
De Luke Ready Mix Corp. v R. — Misc2d —, 161 NYS2d 626.
Rodriguez v J. (Tex Civ App) 289 SW2d 316.

84 ALR 123–129

U. S. v W. M. Corp. (DC Ark) 134 F Supp 898.
Burwell v. P. L. Co. (Miss) 70 So2d 71.

84 ALR 147–165

Selman v. B. (Ala) 72 So2d 704.
Sliman Realty Corp. v. S. E. (La) 73 So2d 447.
Hancock v. C. (Mo App) 267 SW 2d 36.
Appelget v. V. H. (NJ Super Ch) 131 A2d 20.
Smith Builders Supply, Inc. v D. (NC) 97 SE2d 767.

84 ALR 180–184

Superseded 1 ALR2d 1101.✦

84 ALR 188–189

Leslie v R. (Kan) 295 P2d 1076.
Gilmore v S. (La App) 79 So2d 192.
Sprong v. P. E. A. (NH) 106 A2d 189.

84 ALR 197–211

J. Ehrlich Realty Co. v D. (Del Ch) 124 A2d 732 (citing anno).
Dietman v H. (Ill) 126 NE2d 22.
Lawrenceville v M. (Ill) 126 NE 2d 671.
Ballard County v. C. S. B. (Ky) 261 SW2d 420.
Board of Equalization v. O. (Ky) 264 SW2d 651.
Anderson Bros. Corp. v S. (Miss) 85 So2d 767.
May Dept. Stores Co. v S. T. C. (Mo) 308 SW2d 748.
Gamboni v O. C. 159 Neb 417. 67 NW2d 489.
Peter Kiewit Sons' Co. v D. C. 161 Neb 93, 72 NW2d 415.
Arlington v C. (Tex) 271 SW2d 414.
Arlington v. C. (Tex Civ App) 263 SW2d 209.

84 ALR 220–249

Snyder v L. V. R. Co. (DC Pa) 143 F Supp 680.
Halada v L. P. 132 Cal App2d 788, 283 P2d 42.
Zuber v N. P. R. Co. (Minn) 74 NW2d 641.
Anderson v E. (Neb) 83 NW2d 59.
Guzzi v J. C. P. & L. Co. 36 NJ Super 255, 115 A2d 629.

Re Barnes' Will (App Div) 134 NYS2d 679.
Ackerman v. F. (ND) 54 NW2d 734.
Ross v. T. E. I. Asso. (Tex) 267 SW2d 541.

84 ALR 252–265

Cold Metal Process Co. v R. S. Corp. (CA Ohio) 233 F2d 828.
Kederick v H (DC Alaska) 141 F Supp 633.
Trophy Productions v S. (DC Cal) 17 FRD 416.
Pigg v B. (Idaho) 314 P2d 609.
Shira v C. N. Co. (Nev) 320 P2d 426.
Urquhart v. McE. 204 Misc 426. 126 NYS2d 539.
Grindle v W. F. M. (Sup) 135 NYS2d 21.
Bouche v W. (Or) 293 P2d 203. (citing anno)
Nash v G. (SC) 101 SE2d 283.
Midwest Broadcasting Co. v D. H. Co. (Wis) 78 NW2d 898.

84 ALR 271–278

Superseded 132 ALR 142.✦

84 ALR 281–286

Turner v P. (Idaho) 289 P2d 608.
Barango v E. L. H. C. Co. (Ill App) 138 NE2d 829.
Brandenburg v. B. (Ind App) 114 NE2d 643.
Banberry v. L. (Kan) 244 P2d 202.
Selby v. T. (NM) 249 P2d 498.
Adcox v. A. (NC) 70 SE2d 837.
Smith v S. 98 Ohio App 1, 127 NE2d 637.

84 ALR 294–298

Pacific American Fisheries v. M. (DC Alaska) 108 F Supp 133.
Royal Indem. Co. v B. of E. of M. S. (DC NC) 137 F Supp 890.
Halton Tractor Co. v U. S. (DC Cal) 141 F Supp 411.
Ketchikan Packing Co. v K. (DC Alaska) 150 F Supp 755.
Southern Liquid Gas Co. v. D (Ala) 44 So2d 744.
Title Ins. & Trust Co. v F. T. Bd. 145 Cal App2d 60, 302 P2d 79.
Davis v. C. & C. of D. (Colo) 207 P2d 1185.
Brink v. K. C. (Mo) 221 SW2d 490.
Bucino v. M. 12 NJ 330, 96 A2d 669.
Mercury Mach. Importing Corp. v N. Y. 3 NY2d 418, 165 NYS 2d 517, 144 NE2d 400.
Albert Boris Leasing Corp. v N. Y. (App Div) 136 NYS2d 46.
U. S. Envelope Co. v N. Y. 2 App Div2d 343, 155 NYS2d 816.
Whitehall Pharmacal Co. v N. Y. 10 Misc2d 548, 169 NYS2d 543.
Wampler's Estate (Ohio App) 103 NE2d 303, 60 OL Abs 593.
Sullivan v O. T. C. (Okla) 283 P2d 521 (citing anno).
Central Transp. Co. v A. (Tenn) 305 SW2d 940.
State v A. P. Co. (Tex) 286 SW 2d 110.
State v A. P. Co. (Tex Civ App) 279 SW2d 409.
American Steel & Wire Co. of N. J. v S. 49 Wash2d 419, 302 P2d 207.
Yawkey Bissell Corp. v L. 261 Wis 524, 53 NW2d 174.

---

84 ALR 299–302

Higgins v. H. (Sup) 119 NYS2d 103.

84 ALR 309–319

Supplemented 156 ALR 1356.✦

84 ALR 324–329

Nagel v T. (Tex Civ App) 275 SW2d 561.
Grindstaff v T. (Tex Civ App) 304 SW2d 270.

84 ALR 337–347

Fowler v. R. (CA DC) 196 F2d 25.
Freeman v F. (Ariz) 291 P2d 795. (citing anno)
People ex rel. Ponak v L. 7 Ill 2d 156, 130 NE2d 190.
Ex parte Grabel (Ky) 248 SW2d 343.
Willin v. S. of W. C. (Md) 95 A 2d 87.
Hayes v. O'C. (Mo App) 263 SW 2d 66.
Thomas v. O'B. (NH) 95 A2d 120.
Ex parte Cohen 12 NJ 362, 96 A2d 794.
Foley v. S. (NJ Super AD) 108 A2d 24.
Ex parte Jackson (Okla Crim App) 262 P2d 722.
Com. ex rel. Heiss v R. 384 Pa 36, 119 A2d 237.
Commonwealth ex rel. Dronsfield v H. (Pa) 135 A2d 757.
Ex parte Quale (Tex Crim App) 298 SW2d 174.
Ex parte Shirley (Tex Crim App) 299 SW2d 701.

84 ALR 355–361

Superseded 143 ALR 548.✦

84 ALR 366–370

Zuber v. Z. 93 Ohio App 195, 112 NE2d 688.

84 ALR 376–378

Dodson v. U. S. (CA Ky) 215 F 2d 196.
Blassingame v U. S. (CA Wash) 220 F2d 25.
Wright v U. S. (CA Ga) 243 F2d 569.

84 ALR 383–386

Woolsey v U. S. (DC NY) 138 F Supp 952.
Connelly v B. of A. N. T. & S. Asso. 138 Cal App2d 303, 291 P2d 501.
Re Lanfert's Guardianship (Iowa) 79 NW2d 187 (citing anno).
Harrell v W. (Ky) 283 SW2d 107.
Coughlin v. C. (Mass) 94 A2d 79.
Dillard v. T. (Mo App) 270 SW 2d 548.
Schroeder v E. 161 Neb 252. 73 NW2d 165.
Guerin v C. 38 NJ Super 454. 119 A2d 780.
Re Russell's Estate (Pa) 123 A2d 708 (citing anno).

84 ALR 389–390

Green v P. O. S. of A. 242 NC 78, 87 SE2d 14.

84 ALR 393–403

Tomlinson v O. G. & E. Co. (Okla) 305 P2d 521.
Wilson v. K. (Or) 258 P2d 112.

✦When Supplemented see later Note and Blue Book under caption of later Note

15 ALR2d 1152–1153　　　　　ALR2d

paper articles in question were of purely informational nature, did not refer to defendant's case, and were not type of news articles that would reasonably be expected to create prejudice against this particular defendant. State v Spraggin, 71 Wis 2d 604, 239 NW2d 297.

15 ALR2d 1158–1160

Relative priority, in bankruptcy reorganization proceeding, as between judgment against debtor for personal injuries to, or death of, one other than employee, and pre-existing mortgage covering debtor's property.

Construction and application of § 116(1) of Bankruptcy Act (11 USCS § 516(1)), authorizing court to permit rejection of executory contracts of debtor in Chapter X reorganization proceedings. 34 ALR Fed 743.

VERALEX™: Cases and annotations referred to herein can be further researched through the VERALEX electronic retrieval system's two services, **Auto-Cite®** and **SHOWME™**. Use Auto-Cite to check citations for form, parallel references, prior and later history, and annotation references. Use SHOWME to display the full text of cases and annotations.

Debt owed plaintiff corporation would not be dischargeable in bankruptcy, notwithstanding debtor's allegation he and plaintiff were in partnership in travel business, and therefore he was not in fiduciary relationship with plaintiff, in light of evidence sufficient to support finding that debtor embezzled within meaning of bankruptcy statute. Funventures in Travel, Inc. v Dunn (1984, ED Pa) 39 BR 249.

15 ALR2d 1165–1193

Guest's knowledge that automobile driver has been drinking as precluding recovery, under guest statutes or equivalent common-law rule

§ 1. Scope, p. 1167.
　　Physical defect, illness, drowsiness, or falling asleep of motor vehicle operator as affecting liability for injury. 28 ALR2d 12.
　　Comment Note.—Distinction between assumption of risk and contributory negligence. 82 ALR2d 1218.
　　Liability for injury to or death of passenger from accident due to physical condition of carrier's employee. 52 ALR3d 669.

236

Motor vehicle passenger's contributory negligence or assumption of risk where accident resulted from driver's drowsiness, physical defect, or illness. 1 ALR4th 556.
　　Evidence of automobile passenger's blood alcohol level as admissible in support of defense that passenger was contributorily negligent or assumed risk of automobile accident. 5 ALR4th 1194.
　　Answers—Affirmative defenses—Contributory negligence—Participation in activities leading to intoxication of driver. 3 Am Jur Pl & Pr Forms (Rev ed), Automobiles and Highway Traffic, Form 1353.
　　Complaint--Condition and status of driver—Intoxication—Speeding—Weaving Plaintiff thrown from automobile. 3 Am Jur Pl & Pr Forms (Rev ed), Automobiles and Highway Traffic, Form 413.
　　Instructions—Contributory negligence—Riding with intoxicated driver. 3 Am Jur Pl & Pr Forms (Rev ed), Automobiles and Highway Traffic, Form 1623.
　　Instructions—Occupants of vehicles—Guest statutes—Definition under gift statute—"Intoxication." 3 Am Jur Pl & Pr Forms (Rev ed), Automobiles and Highway Traffic, Form 1612.
　　Guest riding with intoxicated driver. 2 Am Jur Proof of Facts, Assumption of Risk, Proof 2.
　　16 Am Jur Proof of Facts 569, Alcoholism.
　　22 Am Jur Proof of Facts 123, Physical Disabilities of Motor Vehicle Drivers—Vision and Hearing Defects.
　　Contributory negligence of passenger accepting ride with driver suffering from drowsiness, illness, or physical defects. 20 Am Jur Proof of Facts 2d 667

VERALEX™: Cases and annotations referred to herein can be further researched through the VERALEX electronic retrieval system's two services, **Auto-Cite®** and **SHOWME™**. Use Auto-Cite to check citations for form, parallel references, prior and later history, and annotation references. Use SHOWME to display the full text of cases and annotations.

§ 3. Generally, p. 1167.
　　Recognizing general rule that knowledge may preclude recovery:

Ark—Poole v James (Ark) 332 SW2d 833.
Cal—See Enos v Montoya, 158 Cal App 2d 394, 322 P2d 472; Bradbeer v Scott, 193 Cal App 2d 575, 14 Cal Rptr 458; Cowan v Bunce, 212 Cal App 2d 48, 27 Cal Rptr 758; Godinez v Soares, 216 Cal App 2d 145, 30 Cal Rptr 767;

ALR TABLES

37 ALR4th 10
§ 4 Superseded 74 ALR5th 319

37 ALR4th 382
Superseded 14 ALR5th 695

38 ALR4th 628
Superseded 83 ALR5th 467

38 ALR4th 1219
Superseded 52 ALR5th 195

44 ALR4th 595
Superseded 88 ALR5th 1

51 ALR4th 872
Superseded 88 ALR5th 301

56 ALR4th 375
Superseded 74 ALR5th 1

57 ALR4th 911
§ 3, 7[a] Superseded 98 ALR Fed 124

58 ALR4th 76
§ 18 Superseded 69 ALR5th 137

62 ALR4th 758
Superseded 71 ALR5th 307

69 ALR4th 1127
Superseded 76 ALR5th 289

71 ALR4th 305
§ 3, 4 Superseded 82 ALR5th 443
83 ALR5th 375
84 ALR5th 191

78 ALR4th 435
Superseded 81 ALR5th 367

82 ALR4th 26
§ 14-16 Superseded 77 ALR5th 595

90 ALR4th 586
Superseded 72 ALR5th 403

ALR5th

14 ALR5th 242
§ 48 Superseded 86 ALR5th 397

44 ALR5th 393
§ 13 Superseded 79 ALR5th 409

ALR Fed

1 ALR Fed 295
Superseded 105 ALR Fed 755

1 ALR Fed 370
Superseded 111 ALR Fed 295

1 ALR Fed 395
§ 4[b], 6[b], 7[b] Superseded 67 ALR Fed 463

1 ALR Fed 519
§ 4 Superseded 60 ALR Fed 204

1 ALR Fed 719
123 ALR Fed 203

1 ALR Fed 838
§ 10 Superseded 69 ALR Fed 251

1 ALR Fed 965
Superseded 56 ALR Fed 326

1 ALR Fed 1020
Superseded 111 ALR Fed 83

2 ALR Fed 180
§ 11 Superseded 114 ALR Fed 551

2 ALR Fed 347
Superseded 129 ALR Fed 273

2 ALR Fed 545
Superseded 141 ALR Fed 445

2 ALR Fed 811
Superseded 134 ALR Fed 257

2 ALR Fed 978
Superseded 147 ALR Fed 613

3 ALR Fed 29
§ 15[c] Superseded 125 ALR Fed 1

3 ALR Fed 592
Superseded 134 ALR Fed 289

3 ALR Fed 843
§ 4 Superseded 127 ALR Fed 141
§ 9 Superseded 129 ALR Fed 377
129 ALR Fed 343
133 ALR Fed 229

4 ALR Fed 343
Superseded 92 ALR Fed 333

4 ALR Fed 723
§ 4-10 Superseded 167 ALR Fed 1
§ 11 Superseded 30 ALR Fed 421

4 ALR Fed 1048
§ 12 Superseded 59 ALR Fed 10

5 ALR Fed 246
§ 18 Superseded 133 ALR Fed 549

5 ALR Fed 440
§ 9 Superseded 30 ALR Fed 421

5 ALR Fed 518
§ 4(q) Superseded 132 ALR Fed 147

5 ALR Fed 674
§ 13-15 Superseded 92 ALR Fed 733

6 ALR Fed 906
§ 4, 5 Superseded 120 ALR Fed 145

7 ALR Fed 110
§ 4[b], 6[b] Superseded 67 ALR Fed 463

7 ALR Fed 855
Superseded 168 ALR Fed 143

7 ALR Fed 950
§ 3 Superseded 106 ALR Fed 33

8 ALR Fed 550
§ 5 Superseded 67 ALR Fed 463

8 ALR Fed 675
§ 2.5, 3 Superseded 97 ALR Fed 369
§ 4-6 Superseded 139 ALR Fed 553

9 ALR Fed 16
§ 12 Superseded 30 ALR Fed 421

9 ALR Fed 685
Superseded 26 ALR5th 628

10 ALR Fed 185
§ 3-5 Superseded 119 ALR Fed 589
§ 6, 7 Superseded 115 ALR Fed 381

10 ALR Fed 844
Superseded 109 ALR Fed 488

10 ALR Fed 940
Superseded 111 ALR Fed 235

11 ALR Fed 316
§ 9, 11 Superseded 149 ALR Fed 431

11 ALR Fed 713
§ 1-5, 7, 8 Superseded 110 ALR Fed 626

11 ALR Fed 786
§ 1-4, 6, 6.5, 8 Superseded 117 ALR Fed 515

11 ALR Fed 815
§ 4 Superseded 113 ALR Fed 173

12 ALR Fed 15
§ 8 Superseded 123 ALR Fed 1

Consult POCKET PART for Later Entries

830

COMPUTERIZED DATABASES 7

Libraries are no different than the rest of the world. They are increasingly computerized. In fact, libraries are often at the forefront of computerization. In the not-so-distant past, you would have to wait weeks for information that was not available on the library shelves because a librarian would have to order it for you from another *lending* library. The lending library would then mail the materials to your library, which would call you to pick up the materials. Now, vast amounts of information are available almost instantaneously. A librarian in any city in the country can contact New York, Los Angeles, even London or Beijing, and obtain information that is then either captured on disk or printed out for you.

CD-ROM

In addition to the various online information networks available to libraries, librarians make a great deal of use of CD-ROM products. Even in the most rural of communities, everything from the old card catalog to encyclopedias is housed on CD.

It makes sense for libraries, especially law libraries to be computerized. Just consider what you read in Chapter 4 on case research. Reporters take up an enormous amount of space. One compact disc can hold about 200,000 pages of text-only information. In lieu of succumbing to

the information explosion by building a new, larger facility every five years, a library can install a few more CD-ROM multimedia terminals instead. They are a highly cost-effective way to deliver vast amounts of information without taking up large amounts of space. By and large, they are easy to use.

CD-ROM is the abbreviated version of "Compact Disc—Read Only Memory." This means that the information may only be read and may not be altered by the user, namely you. No matter how you attempt to enter information, none of it will be permanently added to the information on the disc. The information on a CD-ROM may be text only, pictures or graphics only, or may be a combination of text and graphics. Some have music, speech or other sound effects. Others have movies and other video capabilities.

As was discussed before, a CD-ROM has an immense capacity—over 200,000 pages of information if the data is text only. Think of how many pages the average book contains. The average case reporter contains between eight hundred and one thousand pages. It would be possible, then, for 200 volumes of reporters to be placed on one CD-ROM. Think of how much space a compact disc takes up compared to the space one book takes up, let alone an entire set of books. You can begin to see that libraries, regardless of size, are at a tremendous advantage using CD-ROM.

Each CD-ROM has its own search technique, which makes it impossible for this book to show you how to formulate searches. Do not let this discourage you, however. CD-ROM products today are user-friendly. Most give you total on-screen support with a wide range of instructions and help screens. If all else fails and you cannot figure it out, ask a librarian for help.

WESTLAW® AND LEXISNEXIS™

Both *Westlaw®* and *LexisNexis™* are online legal databases, also called computer assisted legal research or CALR. *Westlaw®* is furnished by West Publishing Company and is based in Minneapolis/St. Paul, Minnesota. *LexisNexis™* is furnished by Reed Elsevier plc group, and is based in Dayton, Ohio. Both systems are geared almost exclusively to legal professionals and law students. The online libraries are extensive. They cover everything from cases and statutes to law reviews.

Both databases require passwords to access the system. A lawyer may have a password if he or she has a contract and pays the monthly fee. Probably the most active users of Westlaw® and LexisNexis™ are law students. Both companies provide passwords to each student, professor and librarian for virtually every law school in the country. The students are trained to use both databases, and they generally have unlimited access while in school. Their passwords are deactivated once they graduate.

Each database has its own search terminology that uses a type of boolean logic and requires instruction for use—more instruction than can be disseminated in this book. This is one important reason that access is usually restricted. The other reason is much more practical when a lawyer's client is being charged for research time. The average cost of using one of these databases is between four and six dollars per minute. An experienced searcher can save a lawyer's client a great deal of money.

A good online search may take twenty or thirty minutes, costing approximately $150.00, while the same research done by using books may take two or three hours, costing anywhere from $150.00 to $500.00 (depending upon whether the law firm is charging for an attorney's time, paralegal's time or even a *law clerk's* time, which is a law student working at a firm).

But staying online for hours is usually unproductive. *Westlaw*® and *LexisNexis*™ are prohibitively expensive unless you know what you are looking for with a reasonable degree of certainty. Their greatest asset is speed, and for that you must know how to do an effective online search. It is important to note that even someone who has trained on either *Westlaw*® or *LexisNexis*™ (or both) will not be a good online researcher unless he or she becomes a good researcher in the books first.

While there are other online databases, including Dialog and Loislaw, all of them require subscriptions that are often cost-prohibitive for the average consumer. If you really need information from one of these databases, confer with the librarian. Librarians often have access to these databases and will perform searches as a courtesy to library patrons. Another avenue is to use the Internet, which is the subject of the next chapter.

LEGAL RESEARCH ON THE INTERNET 8

From what you have read in prior chapters, the legal community has developed a very precise method of finding legal materials. If you follow the rules, you have a much greater chance of finding the answer to your question. Although quite expensive to purchase, CALR and CD-ROM are quite precise. In fact, despite the need for search queries, both CALR and CD-ROM use the traditional legal research framework.

Enter the Internet. For a low monthly fee (and sometimes free), you can search the globe for legal materials. Until a few years ago, finding legal information on the Net was a daunting task. The Net was wild and woolly. Most sites with legal information were not indexed in any fashion. Searching for anything specific could be like looking for the proverbial needle in a haystack. Luckily, this has changed.

Within the recent past, much of the Internet's available legal sources have been vastly improved, making them much more accessible. A plethora of websites are available and detailed search engines make finding the materials easy and fast. What makes this form of research even better is that much of it is absolutely free.

This chapter will introduce you to what the author considers the best legal sites on the Internet as of date of publication. A list of other Internet legal sites is listed as well.

OBTAINING ACCESS TO THE INTERNET

This edition, unlike the 2nd edition, will not attempt to explain the Internet or the World Wide Web. Since the publication of the last edition of this book, the average American has become more familiar with the Internet. By February 2002, 172 million people or roughly 62% of all members (2 years of age or older) of U.S. households currently have access to the Internet. (Source: Nielsen//NetRatings Audience Measurement Service). According to CyberAtlas, over one-half of U.S. high schools either offer online courses or plan to. We are a wired society.

How you obtain Internet access is up to you. Many libraries will offer free access to its patrons. Companies, like Juno, also offer free or nearly free Internet access. While America Online (AOL) is still the most widely used and popular Internet Service Provider (ISP), you can also use Mind Spring, Earthlink, CompuServe, AT&T Worldnet, Verizon, and a host of other national and local companies. The author by naming these is not giving her stamp of approval to any provider. The reader should just be aware that there are many to choose from. The goal is to pick the provider that you think will give you the best service you need at a price you can afford. Some companies will also offer DSL (digital subscriber link), cable modem or satellite link, depending upon your location. These usually cost more but provide a faster download.

FINDING RESOURCES ON THE NET USING SEARCH ENGINES

A *search engine* is a program that will allow you to search the Net (especially the Web) for websites that match the information you specify in a *query*, or question. Search engines are necessary because if you use a good search query, they will provide you with a wealth of good information. Otherwise, you will have to hunt and peck your way through the Internet and if that is not a completely impossible task, it is tremendously time-consuming.

That is not to say that a good query will always yield excellent results. It will not. Search engines often provide what can only be called garbage, as well as good information. This is the frustrating aspect of using search engines. What you think is a good, tight query, might yield 10,000 or more results, many of which have absolutely nothing to do with what you need. Some search engines will find personal homepages as well as serious research websites. Others find websites that are merely advertisements for consumer and business products. Some find both.

Anyone who uses the Internet for any length of time develops a preference for which search engine to use. Ask your friends and colleagues which search engines they prefer and get the addresses from them. You might find an engine you have never heard of before.

Another method is to click on "search" in either Netscape or Internet Explorer. Doing this will take you to a web page that will allow you to enter a search query. Internet Explorer uses it's own search engine, called "search companion" (author is using Windows XP) and Netscape links you to Altavista.

Following is a list of common Internet search engines and their URLs. What is most important is that on the Internet, sites come and go rather quickly so if you cannot connect to a site because you get a "site not available" or "site not found" message, the site may have been moved or may no longer exist. It happens. Just move on to your next choice.

GENERAL SEARCH ENGINES
(in no particular order)

Alta Vista:	www.altavista.com
Dogpile:	www.dogpile.com
Lycos:	www.lycos.com
Yahoo:	www.yahoo.com
Hotbot:	www.hotbot.com
	(part of the Lycos family)
Northern Light:	www.northernlight.com
Google:	www.google.com
Infoseek:	www.infoseek.com
	(part of the go.com family)
Metacrawler:	www.metacrawler.com
Mamma:	www.mamma.com

LEGAL SEARCH ENGINES:
(in no particular order)

Law Crawler:	www.lawcrawler.com
Law Guru:	www.lawguru.com
(access to over 250 legal search engines and tools)	
Law Street:	www.lawstreet.com
Heiros Gamos	www.hg.org
'Lectric Law Library	www.lectlaw.com
Law Runner	www.lawrunner.com
Internet LegalResource Guide	www.ilrg.com
Indiana University WWW Virtual Library	www.law.indiana.edu/v-lib

FINDING LEGAL RESOURCES ON THE NET

As previously stated, finding legal resources on the net has become much easier. If anyone tells you that it is nearly impossible, ask if he or she has tried recently, even in the last six months. The differences in less than year's time have been spectacular.

The biggest reasons for the differences are threefold. The first reason is the increase in the number of legal websites. Some of these sites are inclusive, that is they provide the information directly on that web page. Other sites act as legal search engines. Plug in the information you require and the site's search engine will connect you to the proper legal Web page in the blink of an eye. This is a particularly nice feature because you will not have to keep track of every legal site you find. Just keep track of the legal search engine information and let it do the rest for you.

The second reason is that the individual websites have refined their searching techniques. At one time, if you wanted to find a Supreme Court case, you had to literally hunt and peck for it. Now, some sites allow you to find it by volume and page; case name; and even keyword search. This is a vast improvement. In fact, many legal sites now provide for keyword search, a vital tool for finding anything using a computer unless you want to spend hours browsing list upon list. Nobody wants to do that and most of us do not have the time.

The third reason for the improvements in finding legal research on the Internet has to do with the increase in the information available. The increase has been enormous. For example, you can now access United States Supreme Court cases back to the 1800s. You can find state statutes online and up-to-date. No need to trudge to a law library. No need to pay for CD-ROM or CALR.

Another wonderful point about using the Internet for finding legal resources is that you can save all of it immediately to your computer's hard drive or to a floppy disk and access it when it's convenient for you. No need to print it immediately.

Following are legal websites that the author believes are winners, as well as other Internet sites with access to legal information. The list is far from exhaustive. Keep in mind, that the Internet changes on a daily basis and that a website that is available one day may be gone the next. It's frustrating sometimes but it is part of the Internet's charm.

Two of the best legal online sites are **http://www.findlaw.com** and the Cornell Law School Legal Information Institute (LII) at :

http://www.law.cornell.edu.

To find Federal cases and codes:

http://findlaw.com/casecode

http://www4.law.cornell.edu/uscode

To find State cases and codes (index pages):

http://findlaw.com/casecode/state.html

http://www.law.cornell.edu/states/listing.html

Cases and Statutes By State:

Alabama	http://findlaw.com/11stategov/al/laws.html
	http://www.law.cornell.edu/states/alabama.html
Alaska	http://findlaw.com/11stategov/ak/laws.html
	http://www.law.cornell.edu/states/alaska.html
Arizona	http://findlaw.com/11stategov/az/laws.html
	http://www.law.cornell.edu/states/arizona.html
Arkansas	http://findlaw.com/11stategov/ar/laws.html
	http://www.law.cornell.edu/states/arkasas.html
California	http://www.law.cornell.edu/states/california.html
Colorado	http://findlaw.com/11stategov/co/laws.html
	http://www.law.cornell.edu/states/colorado.html
Connecticut	http://findlaw.com/11stategov/ct/laws.html
	http://www.law.cornell.edu/state/connecticut.html
Delaware	http://findlaw.com/11stategov/de/laws.html
	http://www.law.cornell.edu/states/delaware.html
District of Columbia	http://findlaw.com/11stategov/dc/laws.html
	http://www.law.cornell.edu/states/dc.html
Florida	http://findlaw.com/11stategov/fl/laws.html
	http://www.law.cornell.edu/states/florida.html
Georgia	http://findlaw.com/11stategov/ga/laws.html
	http://www.law.cornell.edu/state/georgia.html
Hawaii	http://findlaw.com/11stategov/hi/laws.html
	http://www.law.cornell.edu/state/hawaii.html
Idaho	http://findlaw.com/11stategov/id/laws.html
	http://www.law.cornell.edu/state/idaho.html

Illinois	http://findlaw.com/11stategov/il/laws.html
	http://www.law.cornell.edu/state/illinois.html
Indiana	http://findlaw.com/11stategov/in/laws.html
	http://www.law.cornell.edu/state/indiana.html
Iowa	http://findlaw.com/11stategov/ia/laws.html
	http://www.law.cornell.edu/states/iowa.html
Kansas	http://findlaw.com/11stategov/ks/laws.html
	http://www.law.cornell.edu/states/kansas.html
Kentucky	http://findlaw.com/11stategov/ky/laws.html
	http://www.law.cornell.edu/states/kansas.html
Louisiana	http://findlaw.com/11stategov/la/laws.html
	http://www.law.cornell.edu/states/louisiana.html
Maine	http://findlaw.com/11stategov/me/laws.html
	http://www.law.cornell.edu/states/maine.html
Maryland	http://findlaw.com/11stategov/md/laws.html
	http://www.law.cornell.edu/states/maryland.html
Massachusetts	http://findlaw.com/11stategov/ma/laws.html
	http://www.law.cornell.edu/states/massachusetts.html
Michigan	http://findlaw.com/11stategov/mi/laws.html
	http://www.law.cornell.edu/states/michigan.html
Minnesota	http://findlaw.com/11stategov/mn/laws.html
	http://www.law.cornell.edu/states/minnesota.html
Mississippi	http://findlaw.com/11stategov/ms/laws.html
	http://www.law.cornell.edu/states/mississippi.html
Missouri	http://findlaw.com/11stategov/mo/laws.html
	http://www.law.cornell.edu/state/missouri.html
Montana	http://findlaw.com/11stategov/mt/laws.html
	http://www.law.cornell.edu/states/montana.html

Nebraska	http://findlaw.com/11stategov/ne/laws.html
	http://www.law.cornell.edu/states/nebraska.html
Nevada	http://findlaw.com/11stategov/nv/laws.html
	http://www.law.cornell.edu/states/nevada.html
New Hampshire	http://findlaw.com/11stategov/nh/laws.html
	http://www.law.cornell.edu/states/nh.html
New Jersey	http://findlaw.com/11stategov/nj/laws.html
	http://www.law.cornell.edu/states/nj.html
New Mexico	http://findlaw.com/11stategov/nm/laws.html
	http://www.law.cornell.edu/states/nm.html
New York	http://findlaw.com/11stategov/ny/laws.html
	http://www.law.cornell.edu/states/ny.html
North Carolina	http://findlaw.com/11stategov/nc/laws.html
	http://www.law.cornell.edu/states/nc.html
North Dakota	http://findlaw.com/11stategov/nd/laws.html
	http://www.law.cornell.edu/states/nd.html
Ohio	http://findlaw.com/11stategov/oh/laws.html
	http://www.law.cornell.edu/states/ohio.html
Oklahoma	http://findlaw.com/11stategov/ok/laws.html
	http://www.law.cornell.edu/states/oklahoma.html
Oregon	http://findlaw.com/11stategov/or/laws.html
	http://www.law.cornell.edu/states/oregon.html
Pennsylvania	http://findlaw.com/11staegov/pa/laws.html
	http://www.law.cornell.edu/states/pennsylvania.html
Rhode Island	http://findlaw.com/11stategov/ri/laws.html
	http://www.law.cornell.edu/states/ri.html
South Carolina	http://findlaw.com/11staegov/sc/laws.html
	http://www.law.cornell.edu/states/sc.html

South Dakota	http://findlaw.com/11stategov/sd/laws.html
	http://www.law.cornell.edu/states/sd.html
Tennessee	http://findlaw.com/11stategov/tn/laws.html
	http://www.law.cornell.edu/states/tennessee.html
Texas	http://findlaw.com/11stategov/tx/laws.html
	http://www.law.cornell.edu/states/texas.html
Utah	http://findlaw.com/11stategov/ut/laws.html
	http://www.law.cornell.edu/states/utah.html
Vermont	http://findlaw.com/11stategov/vt/laws.html
	http://www.law.cornell.edu/states/vermont.html
Virginia	http://findlaw.com/11stategov/va/laws.html
	http://www.law.cornell.edu/states/virginia.html
Washington	http://findlaw.com/11stategov/wa/laws.html
	http://www.law.cornell.edu/states/washington.html
West Virginia	http://findlaw.com/11stategov/wv/laws.html
	http://www.law.cornell.edu/states/wv.html
Wisconsin	http://findlaw.com/11stategov/wi/laws.html
	http://www.law.cornell.edu/states/wisconsin.html
Wyoming	http://findlaw.com/11stategov/wy/laws.html
	http://www.law.com.cornell.edu/states/wyoming.html

Other Sites:

Catalaw:	http://www.catalaw.com
Jurisline:	http://www.jurisline.com/homepage.cfn
Law.com:	http://www.law.com
US Law:	http://www.uslaw.com
FedWorld:	http://www.fedworld.gov
Federal Judicial Center:	http://www.fjc.gov
Internet Legal Research Compass:	http://vls.law.vill.edu/compass/
Federal Web Locator:	http://www.infoctr.edu/fwl/
State Web Locator:	http://www.infoctr.edu/swl/
Fed Law:	http://www.legal.gsa.gov/
Library of Congress:	http://www.loc.gov
American Bar Association:	http://www.abanet.org
Law Runner:	http://www.lawrunner.com
US Courts:	http://www.uscourts.gov
LawGuru:	http://www.lawguru.com

NOTE: *Pick a law school and you will probably find an online library.*

Putting It All Together 9

Now that you have been introduced to the world of legal research, it is time for you to put all your newfound skills together. You may notice that all the different methods fit together like a puzzle. One piece may not make much sense by itself, but put them all together and you have a beautiful picture—the answer to your legal problem.

Ask a Librarian

As it was discussed in Chapter 1, a law librarian can be very helpful. In most libraries a law librarian has been through college and also has either a Masters of Library of Science degree or a law degree. Many have both, which is fast becoming a requirement for the job.

What does this mean to you? It means that the librarian is going to know where to find the materials you require. More importantly, it means the librarian is going to know how to do legal research and will understand your problem. You will be able to ask questions about your legal situation and not get a blank stare.

It does not mean you can solicit legal advice, however. Even if the librarian is a lawyer, he or she will probably be prohibited from giving you any legal advice. The librarian will be happy to help you find the materials, but you will be on your own when it comes time to interpret them.

Reading this book will help since you will have a basic understanding of the system before you ask for assistance. You should try to do as much research as you can without asking for help. First, you will learn how to use the materials better if you do so without help. Second, as discussed in Chapter 1, many libraries have limited reference help for people outside the legal community. This is especially true of law school libraries, which are geared to the needs of the students and professors.

That does not mean they will not help you. It simply means that the librarian cannot spend hours assisting you with research, so anything you accomplish before asking for help is to your benefit. Just remember that a little sweat is good, but if you find you are being driven to tears, it is time to call in the cavalry. Ask the librarian.

WHEN ENOUGH IS ENOUGH

How do you know when you are through researching? Mostly this is a subjective matter. Do you think you have enough materials to support your argument? If you have all the statutes and cases you could find, if you collected a few *A.L.R.* annotations, a law review article or two, and quotes from a treatise, you may be a victim of overkill.

Face it, if you find a brand new case that is 100% on point with your problem, you are in great shape. But as was stated earlier, those cases are hard to find. Usually, you are in good shape if you can show, either through statutes or cases or both, that your situation is supported over time. In general, if you can accumulate a dozen cases or so, and maybe a statute to support your position, you have done plenty.

On the other hand, there are times when no matter how long you look, no matter where you look, and no matter how much assistance you garner, you will not find anything. Do not panic. It happens. If you have searched high and low and in every nook and cranny in the library and cannot find anything to support your situation, you may have an issue that has never been discussed before. That is your answer. You have done everything possible. Go home. Call a lawyer in the morning.

If you really think it is necessary, you may want to ask the librarian to help you reframe your ideas. That may get you onto another track that is more fruitful. If that does not work, or if you already did that and still came up empty handed, give up, go home, have some dinner and get a good night's sleep. Then think about calling a lawyer.

SUMMARY OF STEPS FOR EFFECTIVE LEGAL RESEARCH

1. Determine what your problem is. Come up with a question which accurately frames the situation. For example, if you want alimony from your spouse you might ask "What are the requirements for alimony in my state?" or "How much money am I entitled to?" or "How long may I receive alimony?" or " May I still collect alimony if I have re-married?"

2. Think up all the possible words to help describe your situation.

3. See if your library has a self-help book, practice manual, legal encyclopedia, or treatise on the area of law you need to research. If so, get it and see if you can find your answer there. This is also a good thing to do if you're not sure of the issue you need to research.

4. Think about whether there is, or may be, a statute pertaining to your question. Depending on the situation, you will then use either a statute (to find a particular law or find cases relating to a particular law) or a digest (to find cases). If there is a statute, it may either answer your question, or its annotations may lead you to the cases you need. You may also want to look up cases separately in a digest.

5. To look up statutes, use the index and find any statutes pertaining to your problem. Read them. Make sure they are up to date. Make a note of any helpful-sounding cases you find in the annotations to the statutes.

6. To look for cases without the statutes, go to the digest and find - citations for every case which may be helpful to your situation.

7. Look up the cases in the reporters. Read them. Separate the good ones you might use from the bad ones you do not and discard the latter.

8. Make note of any headnotes which seem particularly helpful. Also note any additional topics and key number headings which may be of assistance to you.

9. Shepardize the good cases, paying close attention to the cases referring to the headnotes you noted.

10. Read the cases you just obtained through *Shepard's*. Separate the good ones from the bad ones and discard the bad ones. Shepardize the good ones. After a while you may have a pile of helpful cases. Only you will be able to determine when to stop reading, shepardizing, reading, shepardizing, etc. If there are no citations in *Shepard's*, you are definitely finished with case research. Also, shepardize any statutes you may have found.

11. Trouble finding anything? Remember *A.L.R.* Remember treatises and monographs. Remember law reviews.

12. Remember to ask librarians if you need help finding materials.

Glossary

A

advance sheets. Supplemental pamphlets which add new case opinions to reporters.

A.L.R. *See* **American Law Reports**.

American Jurisprudence 2d. A legal encyclopedia covering the laws of all fifty states and the federal government.

American Law Reports. A set of books that report on legal topics of general interest. *See also* **annotations.**

Am Jur. *See* **American Jurisprudence 2d.**

annotations. (1) Abstracts, or summaries, of cases construing a particular point of law. (2) Comprehensive legal writings found in American Law Reports.

appellate court. A court that hears appeals from trial courts.

argument. Remarks or oral presentation made in court by attorneys on behalf of the parties involved.

B

bill. A proposal for a law.

burden of proof. The responsibility of producing enough evidence to support the issue(s) in a lawsuit so as to persuade the judge or jury in your favor.

C

case law. The written opinions of judges in particular lawsuits.

case opinions. *See* **case law**.

CD-ROM. Compact Disc-Read Only Memory. Used to store computer programs.

citation. The way all legal materials are quoted. It is a form of legal shorthand used to give information about where a case or statute can be found.

cited case. The case you are shepardizing. *See* **Shephard's Citations**.

citing case. The case referring to the one you are shepardizing. *See* **Shephard's Citations**.

C.J.S. *See* **Corpus Juris Secundum**.

claimant. Someone who believes he has a claim against another.

compact disc. A computer disc that is capable of storing large quantities of information.

constructive service of process. The act of notifying a person that he is being sued by placing a notice in the newspaper and mailing him a copy.

contempt of court. An act that hinders a court in its attempt to carry out the law.

Corpus Juris Secundum. A legal encyclopedia covering the laws of all fifty states and the federal government.

court opinion. *See* **opinion**.

creditor. Someone who is owed money. The debt may be based upon an agreement to pay or upon a court order to pay.

Current Law Index. A guide to locating law reviews and legal periodicals.

D

debtor. A person who owes money to another.

decennial digests, *or* **decennials.** Sets of digests, grouped in ten year periods, which cover all of the states and all federal jurisdictions.

defendant. A person against whom a lawsuit is filed.

deposition. Testimony (outside of court) under oath, which may be taken down in writing.

digest. The primary guide to finding case law in reporters. It is a compilation of abstracts or summaries of each case in a particular jurisdiction or legal area.

due process. A concept that each person must be treated fairly by the government. The interpretation of this concept changes depending upon the interpretation of the judge. Ultimately the United States Supreme Court decides what process is due, but this can also change from term to term.

E

en banc. When all of an appellate court's judges sit in on an argument. It means "on the bench" or "full bench."

G

garnish. To order a third party to turn over to a creditor any property that is being held for a debtor.

grantee. A person who received property from another.

grantor. A person who transfers property to another.

H

headnote. A brief summary of a legal rule or significant fact in a case.

I

index. An alphabetical listing of subject references with their location in a book or set of books.

Index to Legal Periodicals. A guide to law reviews and legal periodicals.

internet. Connection of computers allowing for an exchange of information. Also known as the *Information Superhighway*.

internet service provider. An internet host. A host is necessary to gain access to the internet. Often charges a fee for access. Also know as an ISP.

ISP. *See* **internet service provider**.

J

judgment. A court document announcing the outcome of a case, often declaring that a sum of money is owed.

judgment debtor. A person who owes money, the amount of which has been decided by the court in the form of a judgment.

K

key number. A method of linking cases on the same point and so you can search legal issues by concepts (only West Publishing has key numbers).

L

law reviews. Journals published by law schools.

legal periodicals. Law-related journals and newsletters that are not classified as law reviews.

LegalTrac. A CD-ROM method for locating law reviews and legal periodicals.

levy. Seizure of property by a sheriff. The property may be physically taken or left in place with a notice posted on or near it.

LexisNexis™. An on-line legal database.

M

modem. The equipment that creates the telephone link between computers.

monographs. Books that only cover a very small portion of a subject.

N

notice. notification of a claim or lawsuit.

O

on all fours. A case that is identical to your case in every way.

online. The link between computers over telephone lines.

online database. A source of information accessed through a telephone connection.

opinion. The written decision of a court.

P

perjury. False testimony given under oath. Perjury is a crime.

plaintiff. A person who files a lawsuit.

pocket part. A small pamphlet placed in a slat, or pocket, in a book, meant as an update in lieu of printing a new hardbound book.

precedent. A court's opinion furnishing an example, or authority, for an identical or similar case based on a similar question of law.

R

regulations. Rules that are promulgated, or declared, by a state or federal agency.

reporters. Books in which case law is published.

Roget's. A thesaurus provides a list of synonyms and antonyms for the work you are looking up.

S

search engine. Computer program which enables a person to find information, especially websites, on the Internet.

service of process. The delivery of court papers to a person, giving notification that a court action has been commenced against him.

Shepard's Citations. A guide to determining if cases and statutes are still valid law, and for finding other sources related to them.

shepardizing. The act of using Shepard's Citations.

subpoena. An order by a court to appear or to produce something at a court hearing, deposition, etc.

summons. A notice by a court that a lawsuit has been filed.

T

topic and key number. A word, phrase or abbreviation, in bold face type, and a number, to which a digest refers you instead of a page number.

treatises. Books that cover an entire field of law.

trial. Courtroom proceeding which determines the outcome of a lawsuit.

trust. An arrangement whereby one person (the trustee) holds property for another person or persons (the beneficiary).

trustee. A person who holds property for another under a trust arrangement.

W

web browser. Software that enables a person to read information on the World Wide Web.

web page. One page on the Internet. A group of web pages will comprise a website.

website. Where information is found on the World Wide Web, or Internet.

World Wide Web. A popular method of accessing information on the Internet.

Westlaw®. An online legal database. That provides access to entire libraries of legal information.

APPENDIX
SAMPLE RESEARCH PROBLEM

This appendix is an example of a research problem. It will give you an idea of how to conduct legal research. This exercise will not give you an answer to the problem. It is only a guide, something to show you the possible steps for a particular type of problem. These steps are fairly universal, however, and you can rely on them to get you on your way with your own problem. The research was conducted for Florida. Research tools are common to all states and this research can be duplicated for any of them.

NOTE: *The symbol § means "section" as in the section number of a statute.*

THE PROBLEM

You visit Go-Mart, your local grocery store, after work to pick up a few items for dinner. While walking past the produce section you slip on a grape. You not only injured your pride, you also broke your coccyx (tailbone), which required surgery. Now you want to sue Go-Mart for your injuries, and you need to know whether Go-Mart can be held responsible.

Do you need to prove what it was that caused you to slip and fall? Does it make a difference if a store's employees knew the grape was there? These are just two of many questions you may need to answer before filing suit. Of course, you should first get an overview of the particular area of law, so you can find out what the important questions are.

FLORIDA RESEARCH

As always, it is important to think about all possible words describing the problem. Some words applicable to this problem are slip (slipped, slipping, slippery); slipping and falling (slip and fall); negligence; injury; and liability.

ENCYCLOPEDIA

When you do not know much about the subject or are unsure of terminology, it is wise to start in a legal encyclopedia (unless you can find a practice manual). Florida Jurisprudence 2d (Fla.Jur.2d) is the legal encyclopedia to use for Florida research.

Beginning in the general index, you would find a listing for "Slip and fall". The topic "Slip and fall" refers you to "Premises Liability". Under "Premises Liability, " you will find "Slip and fall cases" with a subheading for "notice or knowledge of condition, duty to maintain safe conditions for invitees, Premises §32, 33." (See Figure A, page 118.)

Look for the volume with the section titled "Premises Liability" and turn to Section 33. Section 33 is a checklist for foreign substance cases. (Figure B, page 119). Not only does this section of the encyclopedia list what you will need to prove the case, it tells you that the pertinent case digest section is Negligence key number 1096. Remember to check the pocket part inside the back cover of the volume for the most recent information.

DIGEST

We already know that one important digest topic is Negligence 1095 but we will explore the digests regardless.

NOTE: *One case relating to the general topic of slip and fall cases under "Negligence 1095" is shown in Figure D1 for illustration purposes.*

Since we know now that it is a good place to start, let us look under "Premises Liability" in the general index first. Under "Premises Liability" are a few entries under "Slips and falls in general." One that stands out is a subheading of "Floors," which is Neglig 1104(3). (Figure C, page 120). If you are unfamiliar with the topic abbreviation, check the front of the volume for a list of topics and their abbreviations. "Neglig" means Negligence.

Find the volume containing "Negligence" and advance to key number 1104(3). To get the most recent cases, be sure to look in the pocket part inside the back cover of the book. Looking in Florida Digest, 2d however, there are no cases corresponding. (Figure D1, page 121) This happens, as the digest topics will often be the same for each state's digest. A casual glance however, shows that under Negligence 1104(7), which is a related topic, there is a case summary concerning a nursing home visitor that slipped on a grape while visiting a resident. (Figure D2, page 122). The case is Markowitz v. Helen Homes of Kendall Corp., 736 So.2d 775.

REPORTER

If you want to see exactly what the appellate court said, you will need to look up the case in the reporter. (Figure E, page 123.)

SHEPARD'S

Remember to follow the instructions for Shepard's in Chapter 5 carefully. You must look in each volume of Shepard's containing your case. The newer the case, the less likely another court will have cited it. Markowitz is a 1999 case. To shepardize that case, first locate the Shepard's for the Southern Reporter, 2d Series. Next, find the page that says "Vol. 736" in the upper corner. Finally, locate the page number, which is "—775—." Under that listing you will find one case, to be found at 788 So.2d 286. (Figure F, page 125).

STATUTES

The first place to begin a search for statutes is the index. Look up all the words you think apply in Florida Statutes or Florida Statutes Annotated.

Once you have begun the task, you may begin to feel frustrated because no matter what word or word combinations you look up, you can't find statutes pertaining to slip and fall cases. What is the answer? There are none. In Florida, laws pertaining to slip and fall type negligence actions are not statutory. You must rely on case law.

Figure A: General Index to *Florida Jurisprudence, 2d Series*

PREMISES LIABILITY—Cont'd

Reasonable care—Cont'd
  unreasonable risk of harm, invitees,
    Premises § 21
Reasonable inspection of premises, duty to
  maintain safe conditions for invitees,
    Premises § 34-36
Recreational use statute, statutory limitation
  of or exemption from liability to invitees,
    Premises § 49-51
Refrigerators, attractive nuisance doctrine,
    Premises § 83
Regulations, admissibility of evidence,
    Premises § 117
Repairs and maintenance
  directed verdict, **Premises § 132**
  duty to maintain premises for invitees,
    Premises § 21, 23-38
  exterior conditions causing injury,
    Premises § 86
  interior conditions causing injury,
    Premises § 93
  necessity of sufficient time to notice and
    remedy condition, duty to maintain
    safe conditions for invitees, **Premises
    § 35**
  off-premises injuries, **Premises § 5**
Res ipsa loquitur, **Negligence § 173**
  generally, **Negligence § 173**
  burden of proof, **Premises § 115**
  instructions to jury, **Premises § 133**
  status of adults, **Premises § 9**
Respondeat superior, duty to invitees regarding conditions caused by third parties,
    Premises § 44
Responsibilities. See "Duties," under this
  index heading
Restrictions. See "Limitations," under this
  index heading
Right of plaintiff to be on premises, pleadings, **Premises § 101**
Risk
  assumption of risk. See "Assumption of
    risk," under this index heading
  attractive nuisance doctrine, duties
    regarding children, **Premises § 70,
    76-79**
  degree of care, duty to maintain safe
    conditions for invitees, **Premises § 24**
  unreasonable risk of harm. See "Unrea-
    sonable risk of harm," under this
    index heading
Safe condition of premises, duty to maintain,
    Premises § 21, 23-38, 56
Security company's breach of landowner's
  duty, **Agency § 141**
Security guards, invitees, **Premises § 16**
Shopping carts, defective instrumentalities
  causing injury, **Premises § 99**
Sidewalks, exterior conditions causing injury,
    Premises § 85, 86
Similar acts or accidents
  admissibility of evidence, **Premises
    § 118**
  criminal acts, **Premises § 48, 112**
  exterior conditions causing injury,
    Premises § 85
  safe conditions for invitees, duty to

PREMISES LIABILITY—Cont'd

Similar acts or accidents—Cont'd
  maintain, **Premises § 25**
  third parties, duty to invitees regarding
    conditions caused by, **Premises § 44,
    48**
Slip and fall cases
  circumstantial evidence, **Premises § 32,
    121**
  express assumption of risk, defenses,
    Premises § 127
  exterior conditions causing injury,
    Premises § 86
  instructions to jury, **Premises § 133**
  interior conditions causing injury,
    Premises § 94
  notice or knowledge of condition, duty
    to maintain safe conditions for
    invitees, **Premises § 32, 33**
  sufficiency of evidence, **Premises § 119,
    121**
  warn invitees of dangerous conditions,
    duty to, **Premises § 39, 41**
Slippery floors, interior conditions causing
  injury, **Premises § 93**
Social invitees, determination of status,
    Premises § 12
Sovereign immunity, recreational use statute,
    Premises § 50
Stairs and steps, **Landlord § 113, 116**
Stairways and steps, interior conditions causing injury, **Premises § 95, 96**
Standard of care
  admissibility of evidence, **Premises
    § 117**
  child invitees, care required by,
    Premises § 67
  off-premises injuries, **Premises § 5, 26**
Standards
  care. See "Standard of care," under this
    index heading
  conduct, attractive nuisance doctrine,
    Premises § 76
Status of persons
  adults, **Premises § 8-63**
  determination of status, **Premises § 8,
    10-15**
  plaintiff
    complaints, **Premises § 101**
    directed verdict, **Premises § 132**
    questions of law and fact, **Premises
      § 128**
    step-in-the-dark rule, defenses,
      Premises § 124
Statute of limitations, **Premises § 100**
Statutes
  admissibility of evidence, **Premises
    § 117**
  building codes, **Premises § 117, 128**
  criminal attacks, duty to invitees regard-
    ing conditions caused by third parties,
    Premises § 47
  firefighters and law enforcement officers
    as invitees, **Premises § 17**
  limitation of or exemption from liability
    to invitees, **Premises § 49-52**
  questions of law and fact, **Premises
    § 128**
  safe conditions for invitees, duty to

PREMISES LIABILITY—Cont'd

Statutes—Cont'd
  maintain, **Premises § 29**
  trespassers, **Premises § 63**
Step-in-the-dark rule, defenses, **Premises
  § 123-125**
Steps and stairways, interior conditions causing injury, **Premises § 95, 96**
Streams, attractive nuisance doctrine,
    Premises § 84
Streets, exterior conditions causing injury,
    Premises § 86
Strict liability, **Premises § 3**
Sufficiency or insufficiency
  evidence, **Premises § 119-121**
  necessity of sufficient time to notice and
    remedy condition, duty to maintain
    safe conditions for invitees, **Premises
    § 35**
  warning of danger or risk, attractive
    nuisance doctrine, **Premises § 77**
Summary judgment
  generally, **Premises § 128**
  building inspectors as invitees, **Premises
    § 19**
  criminal attacks, duty to invitees regard-
    ing conditions caused by third parties,
    Premises § 47
  exterior conditions causing injury,
    Premises § 86, 87
  interior conditions causing injury,
    Premises § 91, 93-95
  licensees, **Premises § 57**
  negligence, **Premises § 131**
  recreational use statute, statutory limita-
    tion of or exemption from liability to
    invitees, **Premises § 51**
  safe conditions for invitees, duty to
    maintain, **Premises § 25, 30, 34, 38**
  sufficiency of evidence, **Premises § 119**
  third parties, duty to invitees regarding
    conditions caused by, **Premises § 46,
    47**
  warn invitees of dangerous conditions,
    duty to, **Premises § 39, 42, 43**
Swimming pools, **Premises § 84, 89**
Tenant and landlord. See "Landlord and tenant," under this index heading
Testimony. See "Witnesses," under this
  index heading
Third persons or parties
  conditions caused by third parties, duty
    to invitees regarding, **Premises § 44-
    48**
  reasonable inspection of premises, duty
    to maintain safe conditions for
    invitees, **Premises § 34**
  recreational use statute, statutory limita-
    tion of or exemption from liability to
    invitees, **Premises § 49-51**
  trespassers, **Premises § 60**
Time
  necessity of sufficient time to notice and
    remedy condition, duty to maintain
    safe conditions for invitees, **Premises
    § 35**
  statute of limitations, **Premises § 100**
Toilets, defective instrumentalities causing
  injury, **Premises § 99**

§ 33 —Checklist for foreign substance cases

Research References

West's Key Number Digest, Negligence ☞1095

The following facts and circumstances, among others, tend to establish that the operator of a commercial enterprise is liable to a person who slipped and fell due, allegedly, to the presence of a foreign substance on the floor of the premises (note that not all of these facts and circumstances will exist in any given case; the applicability of some of them will depend, of course, on the theory on which the alleged negligence is based):[1]

- existence of duty owed by defendant to plaintiff
  - plaintiff's status as business invitee
  - duty of reasonable care under circumstances, regardless of plaintiff's status
- plaintiff's slip and fall on floor of premises
- existence of hazardous condition
  - presence of foreign substance on floor at place and time of accident
  - description and identification of foreign substance
  - slipperiness of floor
  - presence of foreign substance on plaintiff's body or clothing after accident
- nature of foreign substance
  - product sold by defendant or related to its business
  - area closed to public as source of substance
  - defendant's equipment as source of substance

[Section 33]

[1]Am. Jur. 2d, Premises Liability §§ 554 to 614.

Forms References: For personal injuries from slip and fall on oily substance. Florida Pleading and Practice Forms (Rev), Torts § 28:20.

and fall case. Slip and Fall Due to Foreign Substance on Floor, 28 Am. Jur. Proof of Facts 2d 167 §§ 19 to 41.

Existence of dangerous condition arising from improper maintenance of floor. Slip and Fall, 10 Am. Jur. Proof of Facts 785, proof 1.

Figure C: General Index to *Florida Digest, 2d Series*

References are to Digest Topics and Key Numbers

PREMISES LIABILITY—Cont'd

PROXIMATE cause. See heading
   PROXIMATE CAUSE, PREMISES
   liability.

PUBLIC amusements. See heading
   THEATERS AND SHOWS, generally.

PUBLIC invitee, **Neglig** ⟳ 1037(5)

PURCHASERS,
   Parties liable, **Neglig** ⟳ 1264

RAMPS,
   Breach of duty. See subheading STAIRS
   and ramps, under this heading.

REASONABLE care standard, **Neglig**
   ⟳ 1032

REASONABLY safe condition,
   Standard of care, **Neglig** ⟳ 1033

RECREATIONAL use doctrine and statutes,
   Generally, **Neglig** ⟳ 1191-1197
   Construction of statutes in general, **Neglig**
     ⟳ 1193
   Duty of care, **Neglig** ⟳ 1196
   Fee or charge for use, **Neglig** ⟳ 1195
   Persons covered by doctrine, **Neglig**
     ⟳ 1194
   Property,
     Activities and conditions covered by
      doctrine, **Neglig** ⟳ 1194
     Purpose of doctrine, **Neglig** ⟳ 1192
     Standard of care, **Neglig** ⟳ 1196
     Warning, **Neglig** ⟳ 1196
     Willful or malicious acts, **Neglig** ⟳ 1197

REGULATORY requirements. See subheading STATUTORY requirements, under
   this heading.

RELIGIOUS societies, **Relig Soc** ⟳ 30

REPAIRS. See subheading
   CONSTRUCTION, demolition and
   repairs, under this heading.

RES ipsa loquitur, **Neglig** ⟳ 1625

RESCUE,
   Assumption of risks, **Neglig** ⟳ 1315
   Plaintiff's conduct or fault, **Neglig** ⟳ 1293

ROOFS and ceilings,
   Breach of duty, **Neglig** ⟳ 1116
   Construction, demolition and repairs, **Neg-
   lig** ⟳ 1204(3)

SAFE workplace laws,
   Generally, **Neglig** ⟳ 1204(5-8)
   Frequenter laws, **Neglig** ⟳ 1204(8)
   Scaffolding laws, **Neglig** ⟳ 1204(6)

PREMISES LIABILITY—Cont'd
SAFE workplace laws—Cont'd

   Structural work laws, **Neglig** ⟳ 1204(7)

SCAFFOLDS. See subheading LADDERS
   and scaffolds, under this heading.

SHOWS. See heading **THEATERS AND
   SHOWS,** generally.

SIDEWALKS and walkways,
   Breach of duty, **Neglig** ⟳ 1126
   Plaintiff's conduct or fault, **Neglig**
     ⟳ 1291(2)

SLIPS and falls in general,
   Breach of duty,
     Generally, **Neglig** ⟳ 1095
     Floors, **Neglig** ⟳ 1104(3)
     Ice and snow, **Neglig** ⟳ 1132
     Stairs and ramps, **Neglig** ⟳ 1110(1)
   Complaint, **Neglig** ⟳ 1524(2)
   Evidence,
     Burden of proof, **Neglig** ⟳ 1563
     Presumptions and inferences, **Neglig**
      ⟳ 1594
     Weight and sufficiency, **Neglig** ⟳ 1669
   Jury instructions, **Neglig** ⟳ 1735
   Jury questions and directing verdict, **Neglig**
     ⟳ 1707
   Plaintiff's conduct or fault, **Neglig** ⟳ 1288

SNOW. See subheading ICE and snow, under
   this heading.

SOCIAL guests as licensees, **Neglig**
   ⟳ 1040(4)

SPECTATORS. See heading **THEATERS
   AND SHOWS,** generally.

SPORTING events. See heading **THEATERS
   AND SHOWS,** generally.

STAIRS and ramps,
   Breach of duty,
     Generally, **Neglig** ⟳ 1110(1-3)
     Debris and other objects, **Neglig**
      ⟳ 1110(2)
     Hand and guard rails, **Neglig** ⟳ 1110(3)
     Slips and falls in general, **Neglig**
      ⟳ 1110(1)
     Violation of statutory requirements, **Neg-
     lig** ⟳ 1110(3)
     Water and other substances, **Neglig**
      ⟳ 1110(2)

STANDARD of care,
   Generally, **Neglig** ⟳ 1030-1079
   Criminal acts of third persons, **Neglig**
     ⟳ 1070
   Due care, **Neglig** ⟳ 1032
   Firefighters, **Neglig** ⟳ 1060

NEGLIGENCE

(C) STANDARD OF CARE.

☞1031. Not insurer or guarantor.

Tex.App.–Houston [14 Dist.] 2001. Premises owner's duty toward its invitee does not make the possessor an insurer of the invitee's safety.—Wal-Mart Stores, Inc. v. Redding, 56 S.W.3d 141, rehearing overruled.

☞1037(4). Care required in general.

Ky.App. 2001. Under common law premises liability, the owner of a premises to which the public is invited has a general duty to exercise ordinary care to keep the premises in a reasonably safe condition and warn invitees of dangers that are latent, unknown or not obvious.—Lewis v. B & R Corporation, 56 S.W.3d 432.

Tex.App.–Houston [14 Dist.] 2001. Premises owner's duty toward its invitee does not make the possessor an insurer of the invitee's safety.—Wal-Mart Stores, Inc. v. Redding, 56 S.W.3d 141, rehearing overruled.

☞1076. —— In general.

Tex.App.–Houston [14 Dist.] 2001. Patron was store's "invitee," and thus store owed her duty to exercise reasonable care to protect her from dangerous conditions in store known or discoverable to it.—Wal-Mart Stores, Inc. v. Redding, 56 S.W.3d 141, rehearing overruled.

(D) BREACH OF DUTY.

☞1095. Slips and falls in general.

Tex.App.–Houston [14 Dist.] 2001. To recover damages in a slip-and-fall case, a plaintiff must prove: (1) actual or constructive knowledge of some condition on the premises by the owner/operator, (2) that the condition posed an unreasonable risk of harm, (3) that the owner/operator did not exercise reasonable care to reduce or eliminate the risk, and (4) that the owner/operator's failure to use such care proximately caused the plaintiff's injuries.—Wal-Mart Stores, Inc. v. Redding, 56 S.W.3d 141, rehearing overruled.

☞1101. —— In general.

Ky.App. 2001. Statutes, ordinances, regulations and building codes may create a duty subject to liability as negligence per se.—Lewis v. B & R Corporation, 56 S.W.3d 432.

☞1104(6). Water and other substances.

Tex.App.–Houston [14 Dist.] 2001. In slip-and-fall cases, the actual or constructive knowledge requirement be met in one of three ways, namely, the invitee may prove: (1) the owner/operator put the foreign substance on the floor, (2) the owner/operator knew that it was on the floor and negligently failed to remove it, or (3) the substance was on the floor so long that, in the exercise of ordinary care, it should have been discovered and removed.—Wal-Mart Stores, Inc. v. Redding, 56 S.W.3d 141, rehearing overruled.

Generally, a plaintiff establishes constructive knowledge of a dangerous condition with evidence that the foreign substance was on the floor so long that it should have been discovered and removed in the exercise of ordinary care.—Id.

(92)

XVIII. ACTIONS.

(C) EVIDENCE.

5. WEIGHT AND SUFFICIENCY.

☞1670. —— Buildings and other structures.

Tex.App.–Houston [14 Dist.] 2001. More than scintilla of evidence existed from which jury could determine that store had actual knowledge of wet mist on floor, which allegedly caused patron to slip and injure herself, for purposes of patron's premises liability action against store, where store patron testified that immediately after she slipped she looked down at floor and noticed it was covered with mist of water, patron immediately told employee, who was standing just beyond area where incident occurred about 15 feet inside entrance, patron testified that employee told patron that she was worried that somebody was going to get hurt because it had been like that all day, and that before accident, floor had been mopped several times.—Wal-Mart Stores, Inc. v. Redding, 56 S.W.3d 141, rehearing overruled.

Evidence was factually sufficient to support jury's implied finding that prior to patron's arrival, store had actual knowledge of dangerous condition created by wet mist on floor where patron slipped, even though manager testified to periodic efforts to ameliorate moisture brought into store by customers, and to warn customers about dangerous condition, which was relevant to issue of whether store exercised reasonable care to reduce or eliminate risk, where patron testified that employee told her she was worried someone might slip, and manager testified that because of weather, store had placed floor mats and caution cones in vestibule area, he did not know if safety cones were out in area where patron slipped, that floor in area where patron slipped had been mopped at various times during day, and mats were not where slip occurred.—Id.

Figure D2: *Florida Digest, 2d Series* (pocket part supplement)

NEGLIGENCE

XVII. PREMISES LIABILITY.

(D) BREACH OF DUTY.

⚷1086. **Defect or dangerous conditions generally.**
Fla.App. 1 Dist. 2000. Possessor of land cannot refuse to correct a dangerous condition on land for which it is responsible when that danger is expressly called to its attention and then escape all liability as a matter of law when that dangerous condition foreseeably results in injury to another.—Cusick ex rel. Cusick v. City of Neptune Beach, 765 So.2d 175.

⚷1088. —— **In general.**
Fla.App. 1 Dist. 2000. Possessor of land cannot refuse to correct a dangerous condition on land for which it is responsible when that danger is expressly called to its attention and then escape all liability as a matter of law when that dangerous condition foreseeably results in injury to another.—Cusick ex rel. Cusick v. City of Neptune Beach. 765 So.2d 175.
Fla.App. 4 Dist. 1999. In a slip and fall action, the plaintiff must generally prove that the owner of the premises had actual or constructive knowledge of the causative condition.—Soriano v. B & B Cash Grocery Stores, Inc., 757 So.2d 514. review granted 744 So.2d 456.

⚷1089. —— **Constructive notice.**
Fla.App. 3 Dist. 2000. Constructive notice of a dangerous condition may be shown by presenting evidence that the condition existed for such a length of time that, in exercise of ordinary care, the defendant should have known of the condition.—Cisneros v. Costco Wholesale Corp., 754 So.2d 819.

⚷1104(4). **Inequalities in surface.**
Fla.App. 2 Dist. 1998. Customer could not recover from store for injuries sustained in trip and fall allegedly caused by strip of material protruding from area between two floor surfaces, where there was no evidence that store had actual or constructive notice of offending condition, or that floor was improperly installed or maintained.—Fogel v. Staples the Office Superstore, Inc., 750 So.2d 30.

⚷1104(6). **Water and other substances.**
Fla.App. 5 Dist. 2000. Store patron who slipped and fell on egg on floor was required to prove that store, through its employees, could be charged with constructive knowledge of the dangerous condition, given absence of proof or suggestion that store employee caused egg to fall or that anyone actually saw egg before patron fell.—Hussain v. Winn Dixie Stores, Inc., 765 So.2d 141, rehearing denied.

⚷1104(7). **Objects and debris.**
Fla.App. 3 Dist. 1999. Nursing home visitor could not prove that nursing home had actual or constructive knowledge of grape on floor and thus nursing home was not liable for visitor's slip and fall on grape; there was no evidence that because three nurses were in vicinity they saw or should have seen grape, there was no evidence to suggest that grape was on floor for a length of time that would place nursing home on reasonable notice of its existence, and there was no evidence of previous instance where food substance was on floor and resulted in injury so as to put nursing home on notice that it should be looking for food.—Markowitz v. Helen Homes of Kendall Corp., 736 So.2d 775, review granted 743 So.2d 509.

⚷1117. —— **Elevators and escalators.**
Liabilities of owners to passengers, see CARRIERS.

⚷1119. —— **Furniture, shelves, displays, carts and other accessories.**
Fla.App. 2 Dist. 2000. Store patron established store's liability for injuries sustained when a box containing a van console fell on her head; while walking in a sporting goods aisle, the patron observed two employees transferring merchandise from atop a display to a lower shelf, and as she walked past them, she heard someone say "oh," upon which she turned in the direction of the sound and the employees, was struck on her right forehead, and fell to the floor; as she stood up, she observed a box containing a van console on the ground near where she had fallen.—Wal-Mart Stores, Inc. v. Boertlein, 775 So.2d 345.

⚷1152. —— **Adjacent public ways.**
Defects in sidewalks or other public ways, see MUNICIPAL CORPORATIONS ⚷808 and HIGHWAYS ⚷199; automobile accidents, see AUTOMOBILES ⚷269, 289.

(G) LIABILITIES RELATING TO CONSTRUCTION, DEMOLITION AND REPAIR.

⚷1204(1). **In general.**
Fla.App. 3 Dist. 2000. Building owner did not have a duty to warn air conditioning repair person that there were construction items on the second floor where the air conditioning unit was located, where dark lighting conditions were obvious, it was repair person's responsibility to provide the lighting necessary for the work, building appeared to be under construction, and pieces of pipe on which repair person slipped were there to be seen upon any reasonable inspection of the work area.—Roberts v. Dacra Design Associates, Ltd., 766 So.2d 1184.

⚷1205(3). **Lenders, financiers and mortgagees.**
Non-construction-related liabilities, see ⚷1268.

⚷1205(4). **Architects and designers.**
Fla.App. 4 Dist. 2000. Allegations that architect prepared erroneous design documents with knowledge that owner would supply them to the successful bidder, and that successful bidder would be injured if they were inadequate, were sufficient to establish a special relationship between architect and general contractor that was the successful bidder, supporting general contractor's action for professional malpractice against architect despite lack of contract between general contractor and architect.—Hewett-Kier Const., Inc. v. Lemuel Ramos and Associates, Inc., 775 So.2d 373, rehearing denied.

⚷1205(5). **Engineers.**
Fla. 1999. Homeowner could bring negligence claim against engineers who allegedly failed to detect and disclose certain defects in condition of home inspected, although neither engineer signed contract between homeowner and engineering firm, their employer, where engineers were designated by employer to perform engineering services for homeowner, and both were responsible for performing professional services to a client of their company whom they reasonably knew or should have known would be injured if they were negligent in the performance of those services. West's F.S.A. §§ 471.023, 621.07.—Moransais v. Heathman, 744 So.2d 973, rehearing denied.

⚷1205(7). —— **In general.**
Fla.App. 4 Dist. 1997. Contractors may share responsibility for injuries caused on or around construction site even though landowner retains some possession and control of premises.—Worth v. Eugene Gentile Builders, 744 So.2d 1014, opin-

MARKOWITZ v. HELEN HOMES OF KENDALL CORP.   Fla. **775**
Cite as 736 So.2d 775 (Fla.App. 3 Dist. 1999)

Patricia MARKOWITZ and Robert
Markowitz, Appellants,

v.

HELEN HOMES OF KENDALL COR-
PORATION, a/k/a Kendall Health
Care Properties, d/b/a The Palace Liv-
ing Facility, Appellee.

No. 98–452.

District Court of Appeal of Florida,
Third District.

July 7, 1999.

Visitor brought slip and fall action
against nursing home. The Circuit Court,
Dade County, Thomas S. Wilson Jr., J.,
granted summary judgment to nursing
home. Visitor appealed. The District Court
of Appeal held that visitor could not prove
that nursing home had actual or constructive knowledge of grape on floor.

Affirmed.

Negligence ⚖1104(7)

Nursing home visitor could not prove
that nursing home had actual or constructive knowledge of grape on floor and thus
nursing home was not liable for visitor's
slip and fall on grape; there was no evidence that because three nurses were in
vicinity they saw or should have seen
grape, there was no evidence to suggest
that grape was on floor for a length of
time that would place nursing home on
reasonable notice of its existence, and
there was no evidence of previous instance
where food substance was on floor and
resulted in injury so as to put nursing
home on notice that it should be looking
for food.

Podhurst, Orseck, Josefsberg, Eaton,
Meadow, Olin & Perwin and Joel D. Eaton, Miami, for appellant.

Kubicki Draper and Angela C. Flowers,
Ft. Lauderdale, for appellee.

Before JORGENSON, COPE, and
LEVY, JJ.

PER CURIAM.

This is an appeal from a trial court
Order granting defendant/Helen Homes of
Kendall Corporation's ("the nursing
home") Motion for Summary Judgment
and denying the plaintiffs/Patricia and
Robert Markowitz's ("the Markowitzes")
Motion for Summary Judgment. We af-
firm.

The Markowitzes brought suit against
the nursing home alleging that Mrs. Markowitz slipped and fell on a grape in the
main area of the nursing home facility and
sustained serious injuries while visiting her
mother, a resident at the nursing home.
The Complaint alleges that the nursing
home knew or should have known of the
dangerous condition but negligently failed
to correct it.

After discovery, the nursing home
moved for summary judgment contending
that there was no evidence that the defendant had actual knowledge of the presence
of the grape, or that the grape was on the
floor for a sufficient length of time to
provide it with constructive notice of its
presence. The Markowitzes responded
that three of the nursing home's employees were engaged in a conversation in the
immediate vicinity of the fall and should
have been aware of the presence of the
grape. Additionally, the Markowitzes attached the affidavit of an expert nursing
home administrator who stated that per-
mitting elderly residents to carry food
from the dining room to their room was
unreasonably dangerous. The nursing
home relied on the testimony of the nurses, who denied knowledge of the presence
of the grape, and the deposition of the
building supervisor and the housekeeper,
who each testified that the nursing home's
policy was that common areas are swept
and cleaned several times throughout the
day. The trial court granted the nursing

Figure E: *Southern Reporter, 2d Series (Florida Cases) Continued*

home's motion and entered Final Summary Judgment.

We affirm the entry of Final Summary Judgment because the Markowitzes are unable to prove that the nursing home had actual or constructive knowledge of the spilt grape. *See Miller v. Big C Trading, Inc.*, 641 So.2d 911 (Fla. 3d DCA 1994); *see also Publix Super Market, Inc. v. Sanchez*, 700 So.2d 405 (Fla. 3d DCA 1997). There is no evidence in the record to support the Markowitzes' contention that because three nurses were in the vicinity of the fall they saw or should have seen the grape. Furthermore, there is no evidence to suggest that the grape was on the floor for a length of time that would place the nursing home on reasonable notice of its existence. Additionally, the Markowitzes are unable to establish that the nursing home's method of operation is negligent. *Publix Super Market, Inc. v. Sanchez*, 700 So.2d at 406. There is no evidence of a previous instance where a grape or other food substance was on the floor and resulted in injury to a resident or visitor so as to put the nursing home on notice that they should be looking for food.

Affirmed.

Tessie SCHUSSEL, Appellant/Cross–Appellee,

v.

LADD HAIRDRESSERS, INC., d/b/a Hair & Company, a Florida corporation, Appellee/Cross–Appellant.

Nos. 98–1713, 98–1853.

District Court of Appeal of Florida, Fourth District.

July 7, 1999.

Patron brought trip and fall action against owner of hairdressing shop. The Circuit Court, Broward County, John T. Luzzo, J., entered judgment on jury verdict for shop owner and denied shop owner's motion to tax costs and attorney's fees. Shop owner appealed. The District Court of Appeal, Hazouri, J., held that shop owner's offer of judgment was untimely and unenforceable because it was made less than 45 days before the first day of the docket on which the case was set for trial.

Affirmed.

1. Costs ⚷42(4)

Defendant's offer of judgment was untimely and thus unenforceable because it was made less than 45 days before the first day of the docket on which the case was set for trial, even though case actually went to trial almost six months after it was first set for trial, after defendant was granted a continuance over plaintiff's objection. West's F.S.A. RCP Rule 1.442(b).

2. Costs ⚷42(2)

Statute governing offers of judgment and rule of civil procedure governing proposals for settlement must be strictly construed, as they are punitive in nature in that they impose sanctions upon the losing party and are in derogation of the common law. West's F.S.A. § 768.79; West's F.S.A. RCP Rule 1.442.

Pamela Beckham of Beckham & Beckham, P.A., North Miami Beach, for appellant/cross-appellee.

Hinda Klein of Conroy, Simberg & Ganon, P.A., Hollywood, for appellee/cross-appellant.

HAZOURI, J.

This is an appeal by the plaintiff, Tessie Schussel (Schussel), of a final judgment for the defendant, Ladd Hairdressers, Inc. (Ladd), entered pursuant to a jury's ver-

789So2d¹1186
d 790So2d513
791So2d1128
791So2d1228
d 26FLW(D)
[1623
26FLW(D)
[2016
26FLW(D)
[2453

—89—
s 2001FlaApp
[LX12751

—91—
q 2001FL LX
[610
q 26FLW(S)174

—93—
773So2d623

—94—
Autrey v State
f 789So2d¹1148

—96—
2001FlaApp
[LX16037

—97—
2001FlaApp
[LX³7933
2001FlaApp
[LX9183
f 2001FlaApp
[LX⁴9826
773So2d1238
790So2d1140
f 790So2d⁴1177
791So2d³44
26FLW(D)³
[1458
26FLW(D)
[1657
f 26FLW(D)⁴
[1728

—103—
j 2001FlaApp
[LX13465
j 26FLW(D)
[2350

—106—
De 2000FL LX
[556
De 760So2d947
2001WLR29

—111—
Gr 2000FL LX
[491
Gr 761So2d330
a 780So2d6
768So2d1067

—118—
772So2d564

—119—
774So2d806
o 789So2d402
789So2d¹402

—124—
s 777So2d1185
2001FlaApp
[LX11076
26FLW(D)
[1917

—130—
s 783So2d1208

—133—
2001FlaApp
[LX²12897
2001FlaApp
[LX¹12897
793So2d¹1165
793So2d²1165
26FLW(D)¹
[2237
26FLW(D)²
[2237

—134—
771So2d1253

—138—
771So2d569

—157—
Royal v State
2000FlaApp
[LX9758
764So2d597
772So2d50
778So2d537

—698—
775So2d1017
787So2d¹149

—699—
f 2001FlaApp
[LX10635
d 788So2d1082
f 791So2d544
f 26FLW(D)
[1848

—705—
2001FlaApp
[LX²12260
792So2d²708
26FLW(D)²
[2129

—708—
789So2d985

—713—
773So2d80
787So2d932

—719—
f 2001FlaApp
[LX9199
770So2d297
f 26FLW(D)
[1666

—722—
f 2001FlaApp
[LX6689
2001FlaApp
[LX7475

2001FlaApp
[LX¹13019
779So2d412
779So2d534
f 26FLW(D)
[1234
26FLW(D)
[1380
26FLW(D)¹
[2223

—724—
2001FlaApp
[LX³7459
783So2d1119
787So2d197
791So2d³38
26FLW(D)³
[1378

—726—
2000FlaApp
[LX¹12577
780So2d¹152
780So2d²152
780So2d³152
786So2d1222
787So2d227
25FLW(D)¹
[2345

—728—
s 774So2d26
~ 779So2d521

—732—
~ 2001FlaApp
[LX⁷13434
787So2d930
~ 26FLW(D)⁷
[2437

—734—
Katz v State
cc 771So2d1248

—735—
780So2d192

—736—
786So2d29
787So2d835

—741—
d 2001FlaApp
[LX8774
j 2001FlaApp
[LX8774
d 791So2d491
j 791So2d491
d 26FLW(D)
[1595
j 26FLW(D)
[1595

—745—
De 2000FL LX
[765
De 762So2d917
2001FlaApp
[LX12482
776So2d1018
783So2d1163

795So2d169
26FLW(D)
[2151

—757—
2001FlaApp
[LX4195
2001FlaApp
[LX14480
785So2d500
26FLW(D)
[2483

—761—
c 2001FlaApp
[LX¹9498
c 786So2d647
c 790So2d¹1151
c 26FLW(D)¹
[1681

—775—
788So2d286

—776—
2000FlaApp
[LX²6218
2000FlaApp
[LX6218
j 2000FlaApp
[LX6218
d 2001FlaApp
[LX13794
2001FlaApp
[LX¹14877
~ 2001FlaApp
[LX15748
e 768So2d526
784So2d²1197
788So2d²265
j 788So2d270
j 25FLW(D)
[1259
25FLW(D)²
[1259
d 26FLW(D)
[2356
26FLW(D)¹
[2526

—780—
2001FlaApp
[LX14704
778So2d³1053
789So2d²1231
26FLW(D)
[2502

—782—
Gr 2000FL LX
[535
Gr 761So2d328
776So2d323

—786—
cc 2001FlaApp
[LX11262

—794—
2001FlaApp
[LX7155
2001FlaApp
[LX¹12480
2001FlaApp
[LX13842

j 782So2d899
785So2d517
790So2d466
26FLW(D)
[1302
26FLW(D)¹
[2144
26FLW(D)
[2357

—796—
j 2000FlaApp
[LX6218
f 2001FlaApp
[LX13794
2001FlaApp
[LX16263
771So2d46
~ 771So2d46
c 787So2d175
j 788So2d269
j 25FLW(D)
[1259
f 26FLW(D)
[2356

—798—
2000FlaApp
[LX11640
779So2d¹456
25FLW(D)
[2209

—803—
773So2d³1280

—807—
Baker v State
s 776So2d374
s 789So2d549

—811—
779So2d587

—1150—
776So2d979
j 776So2d983

—1151—
Blish v Atlanta
Cas. Co.
2001FL LX
[2265

—1160—
2001FlaApp
[LX⁶11124
780So2d279
792So2d⁶583
26FLW(D)⁶
[1914
52FLR1039

—1167—
2001FlaApp
[LX11251
773So2d1193
791So2d581
26FLW(D)
[1936

—1211—
j 2001FlaApp
[LX8774

j 791So2d491
j 26FLW(D)
[1595

—1217—
f 789So2d1018
789So2d²1018

—1221—
f 2001FlaApp
[LX¹13457
f 26FLW(D)¹
[2340

—1222—
De 2000FL LX
[329
De 751So2d
[1251

—1224—
771So2d1254

—1231—
~ 2001FlaApp
[LX3353
2001FlaApp
[LX7473
q 2001FlaApp
[LX15677
2001FL LX610
j 2001FL LX
[610
772So2d36
779So2d516
780So2d¹978
783So2d371
26FLW(S)174
j 26FLW(S)174
~ 26FLW(D)
[759
26FLW(D)
[1379

—1241—
US cert den
528US1123

—1242—
2000FlaApp
[LX16978
775So2d304

—1248—
2000FlaApp
[LX17889
781So2d1091

—1251—
2001FlaApp
[LX14896
777So2d²1085
777So2d³1085
26FLW(D)
[2532

—1256—
Hope v State
r 2001FL LX
[1928
r 26FLW(S)651

INDEX

A

ABA Journal, 16
abstracts, 5, 25, 40, 75
adoption, 7
advance sheets, 21, 50-51
advisory opinions, 28
agency, 26, 27
alimony, 4, 17, 24, 77
amendments, 8, 22
American Bar Association (ABA), 16
American Jurisprudence 2d (Am Jur 2d), 10
American Law Reports (A.L.R.), 66, 75-90, 106
    fifth series, 76
    first series, 76
    fourth series, 76
    second series, 76
    third series, 76
amicus curae, 49
Annotation History Table, 78
annotations, 22, 25, 65, 75, 76, 78, 106, 107
appeals, 38
Attorney General (AG), 28
attorney general opinions, 28
attorneys. *See lawyers*

B

bankruptcy, 13
bar association, 7, 13, 15
bills, 20
Blue Book of Supplemental Decisions, 77, 78

C

California, 9
card catalogs, 11-12, 14, 15, 91
    subject, 12
    title, 12
case law. *See cases*
case reporters, 37, 40, 44-50, 108
cases, 5, 8, 10, 13, 14, 19, 37-60, 61, 63, 75,
    77, 100, 107
    cited, 63
    citing, 63
    civil, 37
    criminal, 37
    followed, 63
    history, 63
    on point, 39
CD-ROM, 91-92, 95, 99
cease and desist, 26
CFR Parts Affected, 27
child support, 4
citation, 10, 43, 63, 66, 77, 78, 108
city library. *See library*
civil law, 6-7
Code of Federal Regulations (CFR), 27
codes, 19-36, 65, 75
common law, 6
concurrence, 45, 46
condemnation suit, 6
Congress, 20, 26
Consolidated Omnibus Budget Reconciliation Act,
    24
constitutional law, 14
contempt of court, 44

contracts, 14
copies, 3
copy cards, 3
copyright, 5, 13
Corpus Juris Secundum (CJS), 10
county library. See library
court, 1, 4, 5, 8, 10, 13, 37, 44, 47, 61, 75
    appellate, 38, 45
    circuit, 38
    decisions, 4
    domestic relations, 38
    family, 38
    federal, 38
    house, 1
    library, 1
    opinion, 39, 44-47
    rule, 8
    state, 38
    Supreme, 45
    trial, 37, 38
criminal law, 6-7, 14
criminal procedure, 16
Current Law Index (CLI), 17

D

damages, 6
databases, 51, 91-94
decennial, 41
defendant, 6, 37
Descriptive Word Index, 42
Dialog, 94
digests, 12, 40-43, 49, 76, 77, 78, 107
discrimination, 4, 5
dismissal, 37
dissent, 45-46
divorce, 4, 5, 7, 13, 17, 24

E

eminent domain, 6
employer, 4
en banc, 45
English Common Law. *See common law*
environment, 15
estate planning, 15

F

Federal Aviation Administration (F.A.A.), 26
Federal Communications Commission (F.C.C.), 26
federal law, 5, 13, 48

federal register, 26
Federal Reporter, 48
Federal Supplement, 48
Florida, 9
footnotes, 10

G

Georgia, 9
government, 6, 8, 20
Government Printing Office (GPO), 48

H

headnotes, 5, 40, 49-50, 64
hornbooks, 14
House of Representatives, 20

I

Illinois, 9
income, 5
index. *See indices*
Index to Legal Periodicals (ILP), 16
Indiana, 9
indices, 10-11, 61, 76
Internal Revenue Code, 22
Internal Revenue Service (IRS), 5, 26
Internet, 95-104
Internet Service Provider (ISP), 96

J

judge, 1, 2, 37, 44, 45, 47, 61
jurisdiction, 24, 40, 47
jury, 37

L

landlord, 7
Later Case Service, 77, 78
law clerk, 2, 93
law dictionary, 4, 5
law library. *See library*
law reviews, 13-18, 66, 106
law school, 2, 15, 93
law school library. *See library*
lawsuit, 6, 8, 16, 37, 45
lawyers, 7, 13, 15, 22, 28, 61, 75, 93, 106
legal encyclopedia, 7, 9-10, 14, 91, 107
legal forms, 7, 13, 15
legal periodicals, 15-18

legal rights. *See rights*
LegalTrac, 17
legislative process, 20
LexisNexis™, 93-94
librarian, 1, 2, 91, 105-106, 108
library, 1-12, 14, 27, 62, 91, 107
    city, 1-12
    county, 1-12
    law, 1-12, 14, 27
    law school, 2
    lending, 91
    map, 12
    public, 1-12
List of CFR Sections Affected (LSA), 27
Loislaw, 94
looseleaf services, 51
looseleafs, 51

M

majority, 45-46
Maryland, 9
Michigan, 9
money, 6
monograph, 14

N

New Jersey, 9
New York, 9
North Carolina, 9

O

Ohio, 9
overruled, 8

P

Pacific Reporter, 51
paralegal, 93
patent, 7
Pennsylvania, 9
per curiam opinion, 47
personal injury, 11
petitions, 13
plea bargain, 37
pleadings, 15
plurality, 46
pocket part supplements, 44, 78
practice manuals, 7, 13-18, 107
precedent, 39-40, 45, 46, 61
    binding, 39, 44
        persuasive, 39

procedural law, 7
procedure, 13, 19
property, 6
prosecutor, 37
public library. *See library*

Q

query, 96

R

regulations, 25-27
    federal, 25
    state, 25, 27
rent, 6
reporter system, 47
    regional, 47
reporters, 12
rights, 4, 7, 8, 19

S

search engines, 96-98
security deposit, 7
Senate, 20
session law, 23
settlement, 37
Shepard's Citations, 24, 50, 61-74, 77, 108
Shepard's Express, 62
slip laws, 21-22
Southern Reporter, 63
specialty books, 8, 13-18
state law, 5, 15, 23
statutes, 4, 5, 8, 10, 14, 19-36, 65, 75, 100, 107
subject card catalog. *See card catalogs*
subject index, 17
substantive law, 7
superseded, 78, 79
supplemented, 78, 79

T

taxes, 5, 26
Tennessee, 9
Texas, 9
thesaurus, 4
    legal, 4
title catalog. *See card catalogs*
torts, 14
trademark, 4
treatise, 14, 15, 107
trustee, 11
trusts, 11

U

United States Code (U.S.C.), 22, 27
United States Code Annotated (U.S.C.A.), 22, 25
United States Code Congressional and
    Administrative News (USCANS), 21
United States Code Service (U.S.C.S.), 22, 25
United States Government Printing Office, 21
United States Law Weekly, 21
United States Reports, 48

V

victim, 6
Virginia, 9

W

West Publishing Company, 5
West Virginia, 9
Westlaw®, 93 94

Your #1 Source for Real World Legal Information...

SPHINX® PUBLISHING
An Imprint of Sourcebooks, Inc.®

- Written by lawyers
- Simple English explanation of the law
- Forms and instructions included

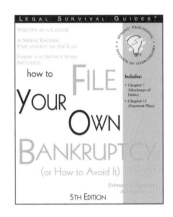

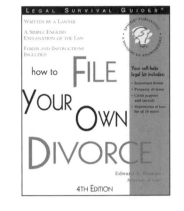

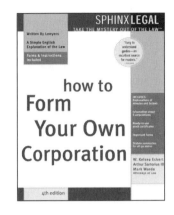

HOW TO FILE YOUR OWN BANKRUPTCY, 5TH EDITION

Whether you are considering filing for bankruptcy or are looking to avoid it at all costs, this book can help you. Includes instructions and forms necessary for filing Chapter 7 (debt discharge) and Chapter 13 (payment plan) bankruptcy and much more!

208 pages; $21.95;
ISBN 1-57248-191-9

HOW TO FILE YOUR OWN DIVORCE, 4TH EDITION

Step-by-step guide for filing for divorce in all 50 states and the District of Columbia with forms. Explains all aspects of divorce including child custody, child support, alimony, and what to do if you can't find your spouse.

248 pages; $24.95;
ISBN 1-57248-132-3

HOW TO FORM YOUR OWN CORPORATION, 4TH EDITION

Protect yourself from personal liability by incorporating your business. Contains a summary of the laws and forms with instructions for forming a corporation in all 50 states and the District of Columbia. Saves entrepreneurs precious capital!

232 pages; $26.95;
ISBN 1-57248-345-8

See the following order form for books written specifically for California, the District of Columbia, Florida, Georgia, Illinois, Maryland, Massachusetts, Michigan, Minnesota, New Jersey, New York, North Carolina, Ohio, Pennsylvania, Texas, and Virginia!

What our customers say about our books:

"It couldn't be more clear for the lay person." —R.D.

"I want you to know I really appreciate your book. It has saved me a lot of time and money." —L.T.

"Your real estate contracts book has saved me nearly $12,000.00 in closing costs over the past year." —A.B.

"...many of the legal questions that I have had over the years were answered clearly and concisely through your plain English interpretation of the law." —C.E.H.

"If there weren't people out there like you I'd be lost. You have the best books of this type out there." —S.B.

"...your forms and directions are easy to follow." —C.V.M.

Sphinx Publishing's Legal Survival Guides
are directly available from Sourcebooks, Inc., or from your local bookstores.

For credit card orders call 1–800–432–7444, write P.O. Box 4410, Naperville, IL 60567-4410,
or fax 630-961-2168

Find more legal information at: www.SphinxLegal.com

SPHINX® PUBLISHING'S NATIONAL TITLES
Valid in All 50 States

LEGAL SURVIVAL IN BUSINESS

The Complete Book of Corporate Forms	$24.95
The Complete Patent Book	$26.95
The Entrepreneur's Internet Handbook	$21.95
How to Form a Limited Liability Company (2E)	$24.95
Incorporate in Delaware from Any State	$24.95
Incorporate in Nevada from Any State	$24.95
How to Form a Nonprofit Corporation (2E)	$24.95
How to Form Your Own Corporation (4E)	$26.95
How to Form Your Own Partnership (2E)	$24.95
How to Register Your Own Copyright (4E)	$24.95
How to Register Your Own Trademark (3E)	$21.95
Most Valuable Business Legal Forms You'll Ever Need (3E)	$21.95
The Small Business Owner's Guide to Bankruptcy	$21.95

LEGAL SURVIVAL IN COURT

Crime Victim's Guide to Justice (2E)	$21.95
Grandparents' Rights (3E)	$24.95
Help Your Lawyer Win Your Case (2E)	$14.95
Jurors' Rights (2E)	$12.95
Legal Research Made Easy (3E)	$21.95
Winning Your Personal Injury Claim (2E)	$24.95
Your Rights When You Owe Too Much	$16.95

LEGAL SURVIVAL IN REAL ESTATE

Essential Guide to Real Estate Contracts	$18.95
Essential Guide to Real Estate Leases	$18.95
How to Buy a Condominium or Townhome (2E)	$19.95
How to Buy Your First Home	$18.95
Working with Your Homeowners Association	$19.95

LEGAL SURVIVAL IN PERSONAL AFFAIRS

The 529 College Savings Plan	$16.95
Cómo Hacer su Propio Testamento	$16.95
Cómo Restablecer su propio Crédito y Renegociar sus Deudas	$21.95
Cómo Solicitar su Propio Divorcio	$24.95
The Complete Legal Guide to Senior Care	$21.95
Family Limited Partnership	$26.95
Guía de Inmigración a Estados Unidos (3E)	$24.95
Guía de Justicia para Víctimas del Crimen	$21.95
How to File Your Own Bankruptcy (5E)	$21.95
How to File Your Own Divorce (4E)	$24.95
How to Make Your Own Simple Will (3E)	$18.95
How to Write Your Own Living Will (3E)	$18.95
How to Write Your Own Premarital Agreement (3E)	$24.95
Inmigración a los EE. UU. Paso a Paso	$22.95
Living Trusts and Other Ways to Avoid Probate (3E)	$24.95
Manual de Beneficios para el Seguro Social	$18.95
Mastering the MBE	$16.95
Most Valuable Personal Legal Forms You'll Ever Need	$24.95
Neighbor v. Neighbor (2E)	$16.95
The Nanny and Domestic Help Legal Kit	$22.95
The Power of Attorney Handbook (4E)	$19.95
Repair Your Own Credit and Deal with Debt	$18.95
El Seguro Social Preguntas y Respuestas	$14.95
The Social Security Benefits Handbook (3E)	$18.95
Social Security Q&A	$12.95
Sexual Harassment:Your Guide to Legal Action	$18.95
Teen Rights	$22.95
Unmarried Parents' Rights (2E)	$19.95
U.S. Immigration Step by Step	$21.95
U.S.A. Immigration Guide (4E)	$24.95
The Visitation Handbook	$18.95
Win Your Unemployment Compensation Claim (2E)	$21.95
Your Right to Child Custody, Visitation and Support (2E)	$24.95

Legal Survival Guides are directly available from Sourcebooks, Inc., or from your local bookstores.

SPHINX® PUBLISHING ORDER FORM

Qty	ISBN	Title	Retail	Ext.
		SPHINX PUBLISHING NATIONAL TITLES		
_____	1-57248-238-9	The 529 College Savings Plan	$16.95	_____
_____	1-57248-148-X	Cómo Hacer su Propio Testamento	$16.95	_____
_____	1-57248-226-5	Cómo Restablecer su propio Crédito y Renegociar sus Deudas	$21.95	_____
_____	1-57248-147-1	Cómo Solicitar su Propio Divorcio	$24.95	_____
_____	1-57248-166-8	The Complete Book of Corporate Forms	$24.95	_____
_____	1-57248-229-X	The Complete Legal Guide to Senior Care	$21.95	_____
_____	1-57248-201-X	The Complete Patent Book	$26.95	_____
_____	1-57248-163-3	Crime Victim's Guide to Justice (2E)	$21.95	_____
_____	1-57248-251-6	The Entrepreneur's Internet Handbook	$21.95	_____
_____	1-57248-159-5	Essential Guide to Real Estate Contracts	$18.95	_____
_____	1-57248-160-9	Essential Guide to Real Estate Leases	$18.95	_____
_____	1-57248-254-0	Family Limited Partnership	$26.95	_____
_____	1-57248-139-0	Grandparents' Rights (3E)	$24.95	_____
_____	1-57248-188-9	Guía de Inmigración a Estados Unidos (3E)	$24.95	_____
_____	1-57248-187-0	Guía de Justicia para Víctimas del Crimen	$21.95	_____
_____	1-57248-103-X	Help Your Lawyer Win Your Case (2E)	$14.95	_____
_____	1-57248-164-1	How to Buy a Condominium or Townhome (2E)	$19.95	_____
_____	1-57248-328-8	How to Buy Your First Home	$18.95	_____
_____	1-57248-191-9	How to File Your Own Bankruptcy (5E)	$21.95	_____
_____	1-57248-132-3	How to File Your Own Divorce (4E)	$24.95	_____
_____	1-57248-222-2	How to Form a Limited Liability Company (2E)	$24.95	_____
_____	1-57248-231-1	How to Form a Nonprofit Corporation (2E)	$24.95	_____
_____	1-57248-345-8	How to Form Your Own Corporation (4E)	$26.95	_____
_____	1-57248-224-9	How to Form Your Own Partnership (2E)	$24.95	_____
_____	1-57248-232-X	How to Make Your Own Simple Will (3E)	$18.95	_____
_____	1-57248-200-1	How to Register Your Own Copyright (4E)	$24.95	_____
_____	1-57248-104-8	How to Register Your Own Trademark (3E)	$21.95	_____
_____	1-57248-233-8	How to Write Your Own Living Will (3E)	$18.95	_____
_____	1-57248-156-0	How to Write Your Own Premarital Agreement (3E)	$24.95	_____
_____	1-57248-230-3	Incorporate in Delaware from Any State	$24.95	_____
_____	1-57248-158-7	Incorporate in Nevada from Any State	$24.95	_____
_____	1-57248-250-8	Inmigración a los EE.UU. Paso a Paso	$22.95	_____
_____	1-57071-333-2	Jurors' Rights (2E)	$12.95	_____
_____	1-57248-223-0	Legal Research Made Easy (3E)	$21.95	_____
_____	1-57248-165-X	Living Trusts and Other Ways to Avoid Probate (3E)	$24.95	_____
_____	1-57248-186-2	Manual de Beneficios para el Seguro Social	$18.95	_____
_____	1-57248-220-6	Mastering the MBE	$16.95	_____
_____	1-57248-167-6	Most Valuable Bus. Legal Forms You'll Ever Need (3E)	$21.95	_____
_____	1-57248-130-7	Most Valuable Personal Legal Forms You'll Ever Need	$24.95	_____
_____	1-57248-098-X	The Nanny and Domestic Help Legal Kit	$22.95	_____
_____	1-57248-089-0	Neighbor v. Neighbor (2E)	$16.95	_____
_____	1-57248-169-2	The Power of Attorney Handbook (4E)	$19.95	_____

Qty	ISBN	Title	Retail	Ext.
_____	1-57248-149-8	Repair Your Own Credit and Deal with Debt	$18.95	_____
_____	1-57248-350-4	El Seguro Social Preguntas y Respuestas	$14.95	_____
_____	1-57248-217-6	Sexual Harassment: Your Guide to Legal Action	$18.95	_____
_____	1-57248-219-2	The Small Business Owner's Guide to Bankruptcy	$21.95	_____
_____	1-57248-168-4	The Social Security Benefits Handbook (3E)	$18.95	_____
_____	1-57248-216-8	Social Security Q&A	$12.95	_____
_____	1-57248-221-4	Teen Rights	$22.95	_____
_____	1-57248-236-2	Unmarried Parents' Rights (2E)	$19.95	_____
_____	1-57248-218-4	U.S. Immigration Step by Step	$21.95	_____
_____	1-57248-161-7	U.S.A. Immigration Guide (4E)	$24.95	_____
_____	1-57248-192-7	The Visitation Handbook	$18.95	_____
_____	1-57248-225-7	Win Your Unemployment Compensation Claim (2E)	$21.95	_____
_____	1-57248-138-2	Winning Your Personal Injury Claim (2E)	$24.95	_____
_____	1-57248-333-4	Working with Your Homeowners Association	$19.95	_____
_____	1-57248-162-5	Your Right to Child Custody, Visitation and Support (2E)	$24.95	_____
_____	1-57248-157-9	Your Rights When You Owe Too Much	$16.95	_____
		CALIFORNIA TITLES		
_____	1-57248-150-1	CA Power of Attorney Handbook (2E)	$18.95	_____
_____	1-57248-151-X	How to File for Divorce in CA (3E)	$26.95	_____
_____	1-57248-145-5	How to Probate and Settle an Estate in CA	$26.95	_____
_____	1-57248-146-3	How to Start a Business in CA	$18.95	_____
_____	1-57248-194-3	How to Win in Small Claims Court in CA (2E)	$18.95	_____
_____	1-57248-246-X	Make Your Own CA Will	$18.95	_____
_____	1-57248-196-X	The Landlord's Legal Guide in CA	$24.95	_____
_____	1-57248-241-9	Tenants' Rights in CA	$21.95	_____
		FLORIDA TITLES		
_____	1-57071-363-4	Florida Power of Attorney Handbook (2E)	$16.95	_____
_____	1-57248-176-5	How to File for Divorce in FL (7E)	$26.95	_____
_____	1-57248-177-3	How to Form a Corporation in FL (5E)	$24.95	_____
_____	1-57248-203-6	How to Form a Limited Liability Co. in FL (2E)	$24.95	_____
_____	1-57071-401-0	How to Form a Partnership in FL	$22.95	_____
_____	1-57248-113-7	How to Make a FL Will (6E)	$16.95	_____
_____	1-57248-088-2	How to Modify Your FL Divorce Judgment (4E)	$24.95	_____
_____	1-57248-144-7	How to Probate and Settle an Estate in FL (4E)	$26.95	_____
_____	1-57248-081-5	How to Start a Business in FL (5E)	$16.95	_____
_____	1-57248-204-4	How to Win in Small Claims Court in FL (7E)	$18.95	_____
_____	1-57248-202-8	Land Trusts in Florida (6E)	$29.95	_____
_____	1-57248-123-4	Landlords' Rights and Duties in FL (8E)	$21.95	_____

Form Continued on Following Page

SUBTOTAL _____

SPHINX® PUBLISHING ORDER FORM

Qty	ISBN	Title	Retail	Ext.
		GEORGIA TITLES		
_____	1-57248-340-7	How to File for Divorce in GA (5E)	$21.95	_____
_____	1-57248-180-3	How to Make a GA Will (4E)	$21.95	_____
_____	1-57248-341-5	How to Start a Business in Georgia (3E)	$21.95	_____
		ILLINOIS TITLES		
_____	1-57248-244-3	Child Custody, Visitation, and Support in IL	$24.95	_____
_____	1-57248-206-0	How to File for Divorce in IL (3E)	$24.95	_____
_____	1-57248-170-6	How to Make an IL Will (3E)	$16.95	_____
_____	1-57248-247-8	How to Start a Business in IL (3E)	$21.95	_____
_____	1-57248-252-4	The Landlord's Legal Guide in IL	$24.95	_____
		MARYLAND, VIRGINIA AND THE DISTRICT OF COLUMBIA		
_____	1-57248-240-0	How to File for Divorce in MD, VA and DC	$28.95	_____
		MASSACHUSETTS TITLES		
_____	1-57248-128-5	How to File for Divorce in MA (3E)	$24.95	_____
_____	1-57248-115-3	How to Form a Corporation in MA	$24.95	_____
_____	1-57248-108-0	How to Make a MA Will (2E)	$16.95	_____
_____	1-57248-248-6	How to Start a Business in MA (3E)	$21.95	_____
_____	1-57248-209-5	The Landlord's Legal Guide in MA	$24.95	_____
		MICHIGAN TITLES		
_____	1-57248-215-X	How to File for Divorce in MI (3E)	$24.95	_____
_____	1-57248-182-X	How to Make a MI Will (3E)	$16.95	_____
_____	1-57248-183-8	How to Start a Business in MI (3E)	$18.95	_____
		MINNESOTA TITLES		
_____	1-57248-142-0	How to File for Divorce in MN	$21.95	_____
_____	1-57248-179-X	How to Form a Corporation in MN	$24.95	_____
_____	1-57248-178-1	How to Make a MN Will (2E)	$16.95	_____
		NEW JERSEY TITLES		
_____	1-57248-239-7	How to File for Divorce in NJ	$24.95	_____
		NEW YORK TITLES		
_____	1-57248-193-5	Child Custody, Visitation and Support in NY	$26.95	_____
_____	1-57248-141-2	How to File for Divorce in NY (2E)	$26.95	_____
_____	1-57248-249-4	How to Form a Corporation in NY (2E)	$24.95	_____
_____	1-57248-095-5	How to Make a NY Will (2E)	$16.95	_____
_____	1-57248-199-4	How to Start a Business in NY (2E)	$18.95	_____
_____	1-57248-198-6	How to Win in Small Claims Court in NY (2E)	$18.95	_____
_____	1-57248-197-8	Landlords' Legal Guide in NY	$24.95	_____
_____	1-57071-188-7	New York Power of Attorney Handbook	$19.95	_____
_____	1-57248-122-6	Tenants' Rights in NY	$21.95	_____

Qty	ISBN	Title	Retail	Ext.
		NORTH CAROLINA TITLES		
_____	1-57248-185-4	How to File for Divorce in NC (3E)	$22.95	_____
_____	1-57248-129-3	How to Make a NC Will (3E)	$16.95	_____
_____	1-57248-184-6	How to Start a Business in NC (3E)	$18.95	_____
_____	1-57248-091-2	Landlords' Rights & Duties in NC	$21.95	_____
		OHIO TITLES		
_____	1-57248-190-0	How to File for Divorce in OH (2E)	$24.95	_____
_____	1-57248-174-9	How to Form a Corporation in OH	$24.95	_____
_____	1-57248-173-0	How to Make an OH Will	$16.95	_____
		PENNSYLVANIA TITLES		
_____	1-57248-242-7	Child Custody, Visitation and Support in PA	$26.95	_____
_____	1-57248-211-7	How to File for Divorce in PA (3E)	$26.95	_____
_____	1-57248-094-7	How to Make a PA Will (2E)	$16.95	_____
_____	1-57248-112-9	How to Start a Business in PA (2E)	$18.95	_____
_____	1-57248-245-1	The Landlord's Legal Guide in PA	$24.95	_____
		TEXAS TITLES		
_____	1-57248-171-4	Child Custody, Visitation, and Support in TX	$22.95	_____
_____	1-57248-172-2	How to File for Divorce in TX (3E)	$24.95	_____
_____	1-57248-114-5	How to Form a Corporation in TX (2E)	$24.95	_____
_____	1-57248-255-9	How to Make a TX Will (3E)	$16.95	_____
_____	1-57248-214-1	How to Probate and Settle an Estate in TX (3E)	$26.95	_____
_____	1-57248-228-1	How to Start a Business in TX (3E)	$18.95	_____
_____	1-57248-111-0	How to Win in Small Claims Court in TX (2E)	$16.95	_____
_____	1-57248-110-2	Landlords' Rights and Duties in TX (2E)	$21.95	_____

SUBTOTAL THIS PAGE _____

SUBTOTAL PREVIOUS PAGE _____

Shipping — $5.00 for 1st book, $1.00 each additional _____

Illinois residents add 6.75% sales tax _____

Connecticut residents add 6.00% sales tax _____

TOTAL _____

To order, call Sourcebooks at 1-800-432-7444 or FAX (630) 961-2168 (Bookstores, libraries, wholesalers—please call for discount)
Prices are subject to change without notice.
Find more legal information at: **www.SphinxLegal.com**